Ephesians

FINDING TRUE LOVE

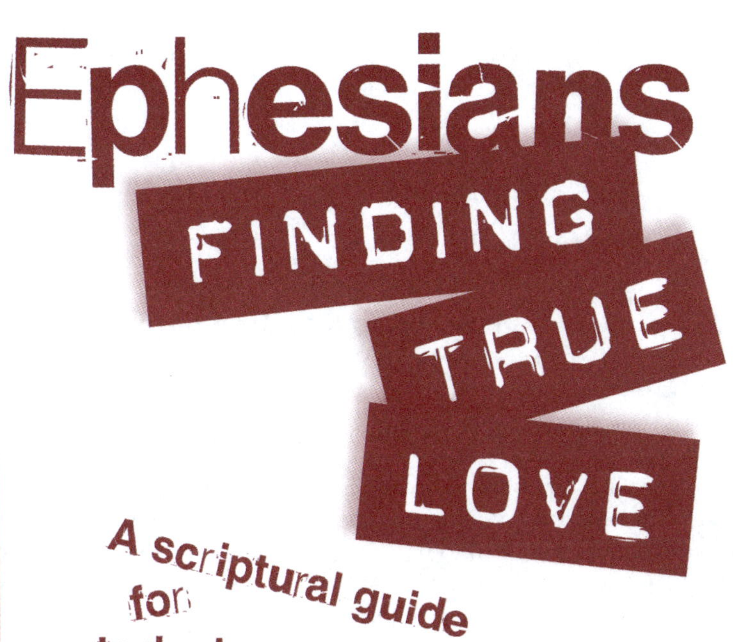

A scriptural guide for today's woman

Sarah L. Howell

Advancing the Ministries of the Gospel
AMG Publishers
God's Word to you is our highest calling.

Heart Stealers Bible Studies
Ephesians: Finding True Love

First Printing, 2008

ISBN: 978-089957111-9

Cover design by ImageWright Marketing and Design, Chattanooga, TN

Interior design and typesetting by PerfecType, Nashville, TN

Edited by Rick Steele

Proofreading by Sharon Neal

Printed in the United States of America

13 12 11 10 09 08 –C– 6 5 4 3 2 1

DEDICATION AND ACKNOWLEDGMENTS

This Book Is Dedicated:

To my husband, Sonny, who shows me unconditional love.
To my daughter, Lauren, who teaches me that love is not threatened by independence.
To my daughter, Abby, who teaches me how to relax and love freely.
To my daughter, Leah, who teaches me how to receive love.

~I love each of you, and your presence in my life is proof that I am loved by God~

Acknowledgments:

Special thanks goes to Jennifer Mulvany who critiqued this study. Your friendship and your willingness to believe in me has meant more than you'll ever know.

Also, I wanted to thank my dear friend, Trish Wilkinson for your encouragement and your listening ear. God has great things in store for you.

I am deeply indebted to my editor, Rick Steele. I respect your writing critiques as well as your spiritual insights. You have taught me how to have a teachable spirit when it comes to writing, and I am so grateful to you for that. Thank you for always speaking the truth in love. And thank you for taking the time to make me a better writer.

To my father and mother, Darryl and Marcie Akiona, thank you both for your encouragement and support. Mom, thanks for being my self-proclaimed publicist and for always having a copy of my book available to hand out. I love you both.

To my in-laws, Charles and Jayne Howell, thank you for your example of true love. Jayne, your unconditional love for Charles is so evident in the way you tend to him. And even if the Alzheimer's prevents him from recognizing your sacrifice, I want you to know I recognize it, and as a result, my heart is forever changed.

A special thanks to my pastors, Brad and Jennifer Evangelista. Thank you for your friendship. And thank you that the pursuit of your vision for CrossPointe Church has inspired me to pursue my own vision. Faith, hope, and love to you both.

And finally, to my Abba Daddy, who told me, "Do not be afraid . . . and write." Thank you for your gentle prodding. Thank you for the way you opened your Word to me in a new way. And thank you for allowing me to steal your heart, because you've certainly stolen mine. I love you.

ABOUT THE AUTHOR

Sarah L. Howell has a special calling to serve women. She has led small-group Bible studies in Phoenix, Arizona, and in Atlanta, Georgia. Her passion for God's Word that was sparked through these studies ignited her pursuit to eventually teach God's Word and write Bible study curriculum. Sarah has a bachelor's degree from Lee University. While studying at Lee and foundering in her dating life, Sarah became enamored with Song of Solomon 4:9, "You have stolen my heart, my sister, my bride; you have stolen my heart with one glance of your eyes." It was through this scripture that she realized for the first time that she was a "heart stealer." Knowing that she had stolen her Savior's heart changed her life forever. This verse has inspired her to write books for women in the Heart Stealers Bible Studies series for AMG Publishers.

In 1995, Sarah was caught stealing again. This time, she stole the heart of her husband, Sonny Howell. Throughout their marriage, they have ministered to youth, young couples, and young adults in Tennessee, Arizona, and Georgia. Currently, Sarah and her husband reside in Columbus, Georgia, with their three young daughters: Lauren, Abby, and Leah. They serve on staff at CrossPointe Church in Fortson, Georgia, where Sarah is actively involved in the women's ministry. For more information concerning Sarah and the Heart Stealers line of Bible studies, log on to:

www.heartstealers.com

CONTENTS

ABOUT THE STUDY

If you're like me, then you probably skip right over this part. But on the off chance you're not like me and are much more attentive to detail, then I want you to know I'm writing this section especially for you. So thanks for taking the time to read it!

If you're enjoying this love story with a group of fellow romantics, then the questions with a heart by them are intended for discussion within your small group. However, if you are embracing God's undying love in solitude, then please feel free to answer the discussion questions with unfettered honesty. (Because no one except you and God will know your answers!)

In addition to the discussion questions, each week contains a specific verse from the passage of study that best depicts the theme for the week. This verse is known as the VOW. or the *Verse Of the Week.* If you're feeling especially studious, then please feel free to commit this verse to memory. But if your scholastic energy has already been exhausted for the week, then just enjoy the scripture.

The *Movie Mania* and *Movie Trivia* sections are for all you movie fans out there. I spent hours analyzing each movie, studying characters, actors, directors, and screenplays. It was both exhausting and exhilarating, and you were worth every minute of it. So I hope you'll enjoy the insights you learn as well as the parallels that are drawn.

And if you don't have time to watch the movie, then don't worry. I've added little vignettes about the movie that will give you a brief synopsis.

So sit back, relax, and enjoy a great love story. And as the Ephesians' love story unfolds before you, may you find yourself caught within the embrace of a loving God.

HIS LOVE PURSUES

Introduction to Ephesians

VOW (Verse Of the Week): "You have forsaken your first love. Remember the height from which you have fallen! Repent and do the things you did at first."	**Revelation 2:4–5**

The Ephesians' love affair with the Lord has always intrigued me. But, of course, I'm a sucker for a good love story. The romance, the disappointment, the fear, and the conquest of love–it's always captivated me. Love is such a powerful force, igniting the emotions, and dictating the thoughts and actions of the poor soul caught within its grasp. And yet, despite its strength and vitality, it grows weak and vulnerable when neglected.

During this introductory session, we'll study the strength and vulnerability of the love shared between the Lord and the church at Ephesus. We'll begin in Acts and follow their love story through the book of Revelation. So grab your Bible and bring your sense of adventure as we journey through time in pursuit of love.

God's Initial Pursuit of Love in AD 51–52

Movie Mania

To better understand this introductory session, watch *The Notebook* and consider the following questions.

- When Allie gets older, what happens to her?
- What does Noah do to remind Allie of their love?
- In what way is God's relationship with the Ephesian church similar to Noah's relationship with Allie?

Allie and Noah would have a whirlwind romance. No friendship blossoming, no love comes softly–just intense emotion. Noah felt it–he did from the moment he saw her. It's what drove him to the carousel and left him hanging there in pursuit of Allie's affections. He only had one summer in which to capture her heart. And he intended to make the most of it.

Paul introduced the Ephesians to the gospel around AD 51–52, during his second missionary journey. Read Acts 18:19–21 to discover what happened.

How did the Ephesians respond to Paul's message?

____

____

____

____

____

☐ **What did Paul tell them in verse 21?**

☐ **According to Acts 18:24–26, who arrived in Ephesus and followed Paul in ministering to the Ephesians?**

Paul may have been unsure of God's plan for the Ephesians, but the Lord had already carved out their destiny. Once initial introductions had been made, God didn't wait for Paul to return to Ephesus. After Paul's departure in AD 52, God immediately sent Apollos to pursue the Ephesians with the truth of his love.

☐ **Has someone ever pursued you in a loving way? If so, how did you respond?**

God's Second Pursuit of Love in AD 53–55

No doubt about it, Noah pursues Allie. At first, she puts up a fight. But the poor country boy who lacks wealth and affluence is endowed with charm. Though he spends his days building a career for himself at the local lumberyard, he has dreams and ambitions, all of which include Allie. But there are two barriers to this unconventional romance. The first is monetary, the second is social.

On his third missionary journey, Paul chose to return to Ephesus. Arriving in the city around AD 53, he was met with a group of believers. Read Acts 19:1–7 to discover what transpired between them.

According to Acts 19:7, how many disciples did Paul encounter at Ephesus?

Were they receptive to his ministry?

Read Acts 19:8–10.

According to verse 9, how did some members of the synagogue respond to Paul's message?

Why do you think some refused to believe?

The book of Acts does not specifically state the reason some citizens of Ephesus chose the path of faith while others chose the path of unbelief. However, if we study the culture in which they lived, perhaps we may have a better understanding of the barriers that kept the unbelievers from a relationship with the Lord.

The events in Acts 19 occurred around AD 53 on Paul's third missionary journey. During this period in history, Ephesus was the fourth largest city in the world, boasting an excess of 250,000 inhabitants. It was a commercial hub, specializing in slave trade and other first-century commodities. Because of its proximity to the Aegean Sea, it became a central port, providing commerce for the rest of Asia. The goods that passed through Ephesus provided great wealth for her citizens, making Ephesus one of the most prosperous cities in the Roman Empire. Her prosperity became so proverbial that she was known throughout the Roman world as, "The Bank of Asia." In fact, throughout his letter to the Ephesians, Paul frequently uses the word "riches," along with other financial terms–all of which would have been familiar to the wealthy Ephesians.

Allie summers in Seabrook, the little island off the coast of South Carolina. Her father's wealth entitles her to mansions in both Charlotte and Seabrook. And while Allie's financial status means little to her, her affluence isn't lost on the local island residents, who know her as the girl whose father has more money than God.

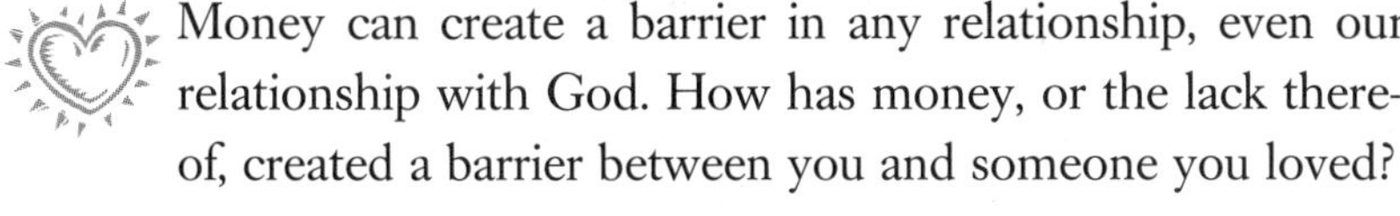

Money can create a barrier in any relationship, even our relationship with God. How has money, or the lack thereof, created a barrier between you and someone you loved?

Beginning in AD 53, God spent over two years pursuing the church at Ephesus through the ministry of Paul. Despite their affluence, many of the Ephesians were receptive to God's love, refusing to allow money to keep them from God. Of course, there were some who weren't fond of Paul's message, but regardless of their opposition, the word of the Lord spread throughout the province of Asia.

Read Acts 19:11–20.

What types of miracles did God perform through Paul?

____

____

What happened to the Seven Sons of Sceva?

____

____

____

As a result of these supernatural events, what did the Ephesians do with their scrolls of sorcery?

____

____

Though Allie may not see herself as a debutante, the society in which she lives certainly views her as such. Her social status is to be revered and her image untainted by the lower class of Southern society. With an income of forty cents an hour, Noah most certainly occupies a space in the lower class. But he loves Allie, and he is determined to pursue her despite the mandates of polite society.

In my opinion, there were two possible barriers to the Ephesians' relationship with the Lord. The first was fiscal, the second was social. The society in which the Ephesians lived centered around the worship of the Greek goddess, Artemis. Though the Romans referred to her as Diana, she was nonetheless a major part of Ephesian culture. The citizens of Ephesus revered her, erecting a temple for her that was so grandiose it became known as one of the Seven Wonders of the Ancient World. Her presence in Ephesus led the citizens of this commercialized city to be very spiritual in nature. But they opened themselves up to the wrong spirits, thus inviting sorcery and demonic activity into their midst.

Acts 19:11–12 records how God pursued the Ephesians in a manner they could understand, revealing himself in extraordinary, supernatural ways. They were awed by his power and responded to his overtures by confessing their evil deeds and burning their expensive scrolls.

Read Acts 19:23–27.

Who was Demetrius?

____

____

According to Demetrius' speech in verses 25–28, what was happening economically and socially in Ephesus?

____

____

____

Artemis and her famed temple made for a fabulous first-century tourist attraction. Pilgrims from around the world would journey to Ephesus, paying homage to the goddess and depositing their wealth into her treasury. However, with the spread of the gospel, the local merchants, whose income was dependent upon tourism and idolatry, began to feel the financial effects of Christianity.

Read Acts 19:28–20:1. What happened in Ephesus?

For a few short weeks, Noah and Allie overcome their social and economic barriers and forge a relationship that will have lasting effects. But summer love rarely lasts forever, and Noah and Allie soon discover that the barriers they had so recently overcome will rise again. Separation becomes inevitable.

God's Third Pursuit of Love in AD 60–62

Movie Trivia Question

- Noah does something every day for the first year of their seven-year separation. What is it?

The riot in Ephesus prompted Paul's abrupt departure. But his absence failed to hinder God's pursuit of the Ephesians. Years later, around AD 60, the Bible reveals God's continued attempts to maintain a relationship with the Ephesians. This time God chose to reveal his love through Paul's writings, composing his words of affection in a letter known as the book of Ephesians.

Read Ephesians 1:1.

How does Paul describe the Ephesians in this verse?

____

____

____

From reading Paul's salutation, what can you learn about the Ephesians' relationship with the Lord?

____

____

____

For the first year of their separation, Noah writes Allie faithfully every day. But his attempts to continue the relationship are thwarted by Allie's mother who intercepts each missive. Her deception keeps Allie from Noah, and eventually Noah gives up all attempts to win Allie back.

Though Noah's letters are never received, God's letter to the church at Ephesus was no doubt received with fervor and enthusiasm. Paul's description of the Ephesians in verse 1 of his letter reveals a body of believers who had remained faithful to their first love.

As the old saying goes, absence makes the heart grow fonder–or wander. Allie's heart managed to do the latter during her seven-year separation from Noah. But in spite of a five-year hiatus from Paul's ministry, the church at Ephesus seemed to be growing more and more in love with the Savior of their souls. No longer relying on Paul to mediate their relationship with Christ, they had attained the goal of every Christian believer–their own personal relationship with the Lord.

But like every relationship, the Ephesians had their ups and downs. Read 1 Timothy 1:3–7 and state the problems occurring in the Ephesian church around AD 62.

Just two years after the letter to the Ephesians was written, Paul wrote another letter, this time addressing it to Timothy, the pastor of the Ephesian church. In it, he instructed young Timothy to discipline the Ephesians for flirting with false doctrines, myths, and endless genealogies. These temptations were causing their hearts to wander from their first love, enticing them to turn instead to meaningless talk.

Seven years of silence. Noah does not talk to Allie for seven years, and then suddenly, she reappears on his doorstep. She has been unable to forget the love they shared during the summer of their youth. But would that love be strong enough to dictate their future choices? And would it prove powerful enough to forge a bond they could never forsake?

God's Fourth Pursuit of Love in AD 95–96

God's final correspondence to the Ephesians is found in Revelation 2:1–7. According to verse 4, what had become of the Ephesians' relationship with the Lord?

The last we hear of the Ephesians their relationship with the Lord is in jeopardy. Though their attraction to their first love had diminished over the thirty-year time span between the book of Ephesians and the book of Revelation, God's pursuit of their affections had sustained a consistent pace. He had not forgotten them, nor was he intending to stand idly by while they forgot him.

In Revelation 2:5, what did God advise them to do in order to rekindle their waning relationship? (Pay special attention to the first word of each sentence. Which two words begin with "R"?)

When Allie walks back into Noah's life, his only fear is that he'll lose her again. Yet many years after their wedding day, and after raising their children, Noah's fear subsides. He loves her without reservation, and she returns that love for as long as she is able.

In the end, it isn't her heart that strays, it is her mind. Some call it senile dementia; others call it Alzheimer's. Whatever the name, the outcome is the same. Now, after a lifetime together, Noah has the memories of better days, which is more than Allie has. While in the earlier stages of her disease, Allie wrote the love story of her and Noah down in a notebook. She gave it to him with instructions to read it to her on days she couldn't remember, promising that her memory would come back as Noah read her their love story. As Allie's disease has progressed to Stage Three, it has become much harder for her to keep her promise. As Noah reads the story of their undying love, he thinks how desperately he needs Allie to respond to him as her husband.

Like the Ephesians, have you ever forgotten your first love? Has your love for the Lord ever waned? If so, what do you do to rekindle your relationship with him?

I wish love were simple. I wish I could ride through life carried on love's emotional high with my feet never touching the ground. But like the Ephesians–who started off strong but then encountered some difficulties–I too often struggle in my affections for the Lord. Sometimes I forget him and forsake him. But over my twenty-year relationship with him, one thing I have learned is that though my feelings wane, his never do. He loves me and pursues me just as passionately as he did at the outset of our relationship.

His primary method of pursuit comes through his written Word. You see, God knows that, just like the Ephesians, we will have difficulty remembering his boundless love for us. So he penned his affections in a love letter known today as the book of Ephesians. Though he used Paul to write the words, they echo the affections of our Savior's heart and reveal the great bounty we receive when we become the object of God's affection.

Inscribed within the worn pages of Noah's blue notebook are written these words: "Read this to me, and I'll come back to you." I wonder what the Ephesian Christians would have done had they inscribed similar words at the beginning of Paul's letter. For when we read this letter, we can't help but remember and return to our first love.

Prayer–*Precious Lord, thank you that you never stop pursuing me. Though I often forget you and forsake you, your love continues to follow me. Please forgive me for turning away from you when the emotional embers of love have grown cold. Arrest my heart oh God, and enable me to do the things I did at the outset of our relationship. Allow me to find joy solely in you. And as I read Ephesians, remind me anew of your love for me and let your love be my most precious possession.*

HIS LOVE PROVIDES

Ephesians 1

VOW (Verse Of the Week): "I keep asking that the God of our Lord Jesus Christ, the glorious Father, may give you the Spirit of wisdom and revelation, so that you may know him better." **Ephesians 1:17**

Day 1: His Love Provides Acceptance

Read Ephesians 1:1–5.

Josh Lucas knows the sting of rejection. When Disney set out to make Douglas Eboch's story into a movie, they solicited the help of screenwriter C. Jay Cox and famed director Andy Tennant. What they did not seek was the assistance of actor Josh Lucas. Disney executives were strongly opposed to Lucas, whose previous roles in *The Deep End* and *A Beautiful Mind* cast him as a dark, weird, and edgy actor.

Cite a time in your life when you felt rejected and unwanted.

Disney argued that their upcoming release, *Sweet Home Alabama,* needed a humorous, charismatic leading man in the role of Melanie Carmichael's estranged husband, not a dark and sinister sociopath. But director Andy Tennant believed in Josh Lucas. Lucas says Tennant "fought so hard for me to do this movie because no one at Disney had wanted me. It was just a battle the whole time."[1]

After greeting the Ephesians in verses 1 and 2 of Ephesians 1, Paul opens his letter with praise to God. But Paul does not merely praise God for who he is, Paul praises him for what he's done.

Read Ephesians 1:3–5 and list the things God has done for us.

After portraying Jake Perry in *Sweet Home Alabama,* Josh Lucas went on to star in such blockbuster films as *Hulk, Glory Road,* and *Poseidon.*

A graduate of the University of Southern California's School of Theatre, Andy Tennant was well known within the movie industry, and people respected his opinion. So when he went to bat for Lucas, Disney execs reluctantly acquiesced. Had Lucas been a mega movie star, he may have failed to appreciate Tennant's tenacious efforts on his behalf. However, as a struggling actor whose support roles had failed to catch the attention of the public eye,

1. Rebecca Murray and Fred Topel, "Josh Lucas Talks About 'Sweet Home Alabama,'" *About: Hollywood Movies,* September 23, 2002, http://movies.about.com/library/weekly/aa092302b.htm.

Lucas recognized that Tennant's endeavors offered him the chance of a lifetime.

How would you have felt had you been in Josh Lucas's shoes in this situation, where the odds are stacked against your winning a key acting role?

In the Old Testament, God revealed his righteousness to mankind by establishing his Law. God's justice requires that we follow the Law and walk holy and blameless before him. But as humans, with a sin nature, we are completely incapable of fulfilling God's wishes. Since crimes committed against God's Law are punishable by death, we are destined for destruction–but God has already gone to bat for us. He petitioned our cause and sent his son, Jesus Christ, to seal the deal.

Jesus lived a perfect life and paid our punishment. He did no wrong, and yet he willingly endured the wrath of God on our behalf–wrath that was justified by our sins.

God fought so hard to make us his, even to the point of sacrificing his own son. God's holiness demanded we, too, be holy. But that is impossible. So God found a way to appease his righteous nature and still make us his own. His endeavors give us the chance of a lifetime.

Not only does God's act of mercy offer us eternal life, but according to Ephesians 1:3, God's efforts enable us to be blessed with every spiritual blessing. The term "spiritual" in this verse does not merely describe blessings that are spiritual as opposed to physical. The word "spiritual" refers to the "blessings produced and given us by the Holy Spirit."[2]

2. Kenneth S. Wuest, *Wuest's Word Studies from the Greek New Testament* (Grand Rapids: Wm. B. Eerdmans Publishing Company, 1953), 27.

Read Galatians 5:22–23 and record the spiritual things with which God has blessed us.

God's sacrificial love grants us access to his Holy Spirit, thereby allowing us to enjoy the fruit of the Spirit. No longer need we sustain ourselves on a diet of depression, guilt, and fear, because our spiritual delicacies now consist of joy, love, and peace.

Our peace springs from the assurance of Ephesians 1:4 which states we are holy and blameless before God–an act we could never achieve on our own. But God chose us to occupy such a position of righteousness, and he used his son to enable us to do so.

However, not only are we blessed with every spiritual blessing, and not only do we stand holy and blameless before God, but now we possess the status of sons. God's actions on our behalf allow him to claim us as his own offspring. He desires us, not just as friends or distant relatives, but as sons.

Ephesians 1:3–5 proves we are chosen, predestined, accepted, adopted, and loved. We aren't just chosen by some USC grad whose resume boasts blockbuster movies such as *Hitch*, *Ever After*, and *Sweet Home Alabama*. We aren't just desired by a director who had the courage to fight for our role in a movie. We are loved, accepted, and desired by the God of the universe.

Job 38–40 reveals God's awesome power. Read these scriptures and list some things you've learned about the One who desires you.

Explain how you feel knowing you've been accepted and pursued by such a great and awesome God.

Prayer—*Father God, I'm yours, not because I should be or because I deserve to be. I'm yours solely because you want me. In fact, you want me so much that you were willing to sacrifice your only son on my behalf. You—the God who established the world, who set the earth upon its foundations, who created boundaries for the sea and commanded the sun to rise—you, dear God desire me. Why Lord? Why me? I may never know the answer to that inquiry, but I am forever grateful that your love, acceptance, and favor have given me the chance to ask.*

Day 2: His Love Provides Grace

Read Ephesians 1:6–12.

The evening promises glamour and fame, but Melanie is less than eager to arrive at Lincoln Center for the fund-raiser. Sitting in the back of her limo she has little energy to do anything but adjust her makeup. She is exhausted, and the last thing she wants to do is be fodder for the local reporters who are enamored with her ongoing relationship with the mayor's son.

When the limo comes to a halt at an unfamiliar location, Melanie is instructed to await the arrival of her boyfriend. This announcement does little to improve her mood. When Andrew finally makes his appearance, she obliges him with a kiss and a limited measure of grace. As he ushers her from the car, he gives her a smile and proceeds to escort her through an empty corridor and into a darkened room.

Melanie's stressful day has drained her, leaving her reservoir of patience alarmingly low. And Andrew's odd behavior is only serving to further deplete her of the precious commodity. Melanie doesn't want to be here. She doesn't want to play the little game Andrew is so intent upon playing. She can tell he is up to something, but she isn't quite sure what it is. And she no longer possesses the energy to speculate his intent.

Movie Mania

To better understand this study of Ephesians 1, watch *Sweet Home Alabama* and consider the following question:

- This is obviously a romantic comedy, but what is this movie really about?

Read Ephesians 1:6. According to the New International Version (NIV) rendering of this verse, what has God freely given us?

Whom did he use in order to provide us with this gift?

____

____

Standing in the darkened room, Melanie is confused and, by this point, has lost all interest in playing games. In exasperation she asks that Andrew finally disclose their whereabouts. At her request, lights come on throughout the room, illuminating glass-covered cases filled with diamond rings. Sales assistants stand by, awaiting Melanie's directives. A stack of light blue boxes bearing the name Tiffany & Co. identify their location.

Paul reveals in verse 6 that God has freely given us his grace, and he's used Christ as the conduit by which his grace is dispersed. Melanie would have never gained access to the diamonds at Tiffany's without the benevolence of her boyfriend. In like manner, we can never gain access to God's grace without his Son, Jesus Christ. God's grace is reflected in a variety of ways, and we will study these ways in the following verses. But before we go any further in our lesson today, be resolute in the fact that every aspect of God's grace stems from his son, Jesus Christ.

Once Melanie's eyes scan her surroundings, she seeks the face of her boyfriend, but he is no longer at her side. Melanie's gaze moves downward where she finds Andrew on one knee. His appeal is simple, "Marry me." Stunned by his request, Melanie watches as he stands to his feet, extends his arm to encompass the whole room and utters the words, "Pick one."

It's difficult to pick one aspect of God's grace, because his grace is so multifaceted. The word "grace" in verse 6 is translated from the Greek word, *charis,* meaning "benefit, favor, gift."[3] However, God does not offer us a roomful of spiritual gifts from which we might

3. James Strong, *Strong's Exhaustive Concordance of the Bible* (Nashville: Royal Publishers, 1947), 77.

choose. His grace does not require we pick just one. His grace lavishes us with many gifts.

Since Christ is the benefactor of our grace, read Ephesians 1:7 and determine what two gifts we possess in him.

God reveals another facet of his grace in Ephesians 1:9. What has he made known to us?

When Andrew proposes to Melanie, he makes his plans for the future known. In a previous scene in the movie, Melanie's friend alludes to Andrew's matrimonial notions, but Melanie remains unsure of his intentions until the very moment he reveals them to her.

The prophets and patriarchs in the Old Testament knew God had the notion to forgive and redeem mankind. They knew his grace would one day allow for these benefits. They just weren't sure how God would accomplish such a feat (1 Peter 1:10–12). In fact, mankind was not privy to the mystery of God's will until his grace intervened and revealed to us his plan through the death, burial, and resurrection of Christ. Until that point in history, God's plans had remained a mystery.

Read Ephesians 1:11–12. According to verse 12, why does God extend his gifts of grace to mankind?

The limo ride to Lincoln Center is brief, but Melanie has ample time to convey her wishes to Andrew. She is adamant no one know of their engagement until she has informed her wary Southern parents that she will soon wed a Yankee Democrat. Andrew's soft smile and warm countenance speak of understanding as he gently nudges the diamond onto her finger, concealing it within the palm of her hand.

There is a purpose for God's grace. He gifts us with good things so that we might bring him glory. His multifaceted grace is lavished upon us so we can reveal his good character and abundant nature to the world, for it is through us that he garners praise from mankind.

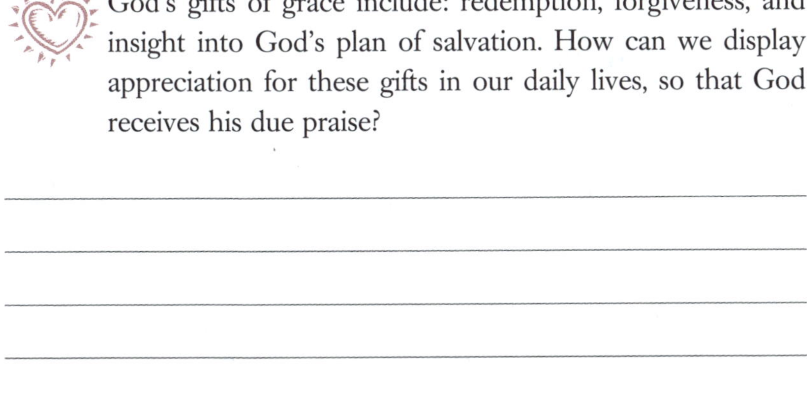

God's gifts of grace include: redemption, forgiveness, and insight into God's plan of salvation. How can we display appreciation for these gifts in our daily lives, so that God receives his due praise?

Andrew's generosity was *almost* denied public awareness because the object of his grace preferred to keep his gift a secret. As Christians, we deny God glory when we hide our gifts of grace. God's love has provided us with grace, and his grace has granted redemption and forgiveness. His grace has given us access to God's cosmic plan for saving mankind. Through his love and grace, we've been chosen, predestined, and adopted. These aren't superfluous commodities that we alone can secure. These are precious gifts that God has lavished upon us. Therefore, we must appreciate them and expose them to others by living courageous lives of forgiveness, faith, and hope.

Prayer—*Precious Lord, I fear I take your gifts of grace for granted. They often become silent trophies upon a spiritual shelf that I alone can see. I pay them little heed as I go about my daily life, failing to give them their due honor. These priceless gifts of grace should be the centerpiece and focal point of my life. So please, move on my heart and allow me to cherish them, for they are reminders of your great love for me.*

Day 3: His Love Provides the Holy Spirit

Read Ephesians 1:13–14.

The sight of the Alabama countryside is familiar to Melanie. Though she'd spent her childhood absorbing the view from the back of a pickup, she now cruises effortlessly past the towering pines and ancient oaks in the comfort of a sleek, black Saab. Today she shows no regard for the flora and fauna of her birthplace. The tires of her convertible speed down the asphalt road as her pulse begins to quicken. It has been seven years since she last touched Alabama soil. Having made a successful life for herself in New York, she had sworn she'd never return to Southern sod. But here she is, breaking her long-ago promise and racing toward a past she had hoped to forget.

According to Ephesians 1:13, we are marked with a seal. With what are we sealed?

____

____

Melanie's hands grip the steering wheel as she glances at the thick manila envelope on the passenger's seat. Its contents necessitate her return to Alabama, and she resents it. Why couldn't he just sign the papers and be done with it? Why not just accept the inevitable and grant her her freedom? Is that too much to ask? Why does he insist upon prolonging this farce?

Ephesians 1:13 summarizes the gospel message by concisely delivering the plan of salvation. Paul's use of past tense verbs indicates the Ephesians had already made a lasting commitment to the Savior. Therefore, all that remained was the necessary paperwork.

In the days of Roman rule, it was customary for a person to place his seal upon purchased goods. That way people would know to whom the items belonged should they be mixed with the goods of others. In this instance, the seal represented not only ownership but also authenticity of that ownership.

God wanted to place his seal of ownership upon the goods he had purchased with his son's blood. So he completed the spiritual paperwork by marking the Ephesians and untold millions of others with the seal of the Holy Spirit. And you know, the comforting thought is that he'll mark us with his seal of ownership as well; all we need do is believe and receive.

Do you believe you are a sinner, deserving death and eternal separation from God?

____

____

Do you also believe that God sent his son to die on your behalf, so you would not have to suffer the punishment for your sins?

Do you believe God loves you?

Do you receive his love?

Answering "I do" to each of these questions enables us to wrap our arms around this amazing gift of salvation. Though only God knows whether our responses are genuine or not, we know that when we call upon him with a sincere heart, he hears us. And when our response to his initiative is marked with authenticity, he places his seal of ownership upon our lives. His precious Holy Spirit is that seal, sent to indwell us and guide us into all truth (John 16:13).

The apostle Paul goes on in Ephesians 1:14 to state another reason why the Holy Spirit was given. Can you cite that reason?

In keeping with the monetary theme used throughout Ephesians, Paul informs believers in verse 14 that the Holy Spirit is "a deposit guaranteeing our inheritance." Much like a diamond ring is a deposit guaranteeing a future nuptial; the Holy Spirit is God's down payment on an eternal relationship with every believer.

By guiding us in our earthly relationship with the Lord, the Holy Spirit gives us a foretaste of what our future relationship will be like with God. The Holy Spirit accomplishes this task by doing a variety of things. Romans 8:26 says the Holy Spirit helps us in our weaknesses. That passage also informs us the Holy Spirit assists us in our prayer life. Additionally, the Holy Spirit enables us to understand God's Word. He enlightens us as we study the scripture, and he causes that scripture to touch our hearts. The Holy Spirit guides us and reveals God's will to us. Every action of the Holy Spirit serves to bring us closer to God. Because of the Holy Spirit's influence, we're able to feel God's presence, experience his favor, and receive his love. Therefore, the Holy Spirit is a deposit, guaranteeing future intimacy with God.

Write 1 Thessalonians 5:19 below.

___

___

___

The New American Standard Bible translates this verse as follows: *"Do not quench the Spirit."* According to nineteenth-century Bible scholar, Adam Clarke,

> The Holy Spirit is represented as a *fire*, because it is his province to *enlighten* and quicken the soul; and to purge, purify, and refine it. This Spirit is represented as being *quenched* when any *act* is done, *word* spoken, or *temper* indulged, contrary to its dictates. It is the Spirit of *love*, and therefore anger, malice, revenge, or any unkind

> or unholy temper, will quench it so that it will withdraw its influences; and then the heart is left in a state of *hardness* and *darkness*.[4]

The dust from the gravel driveway chases Melanie's Saab as she pulls up to Jake's house–their house, although she feels no sense of ownership. The barking dog announces Melanie's arrival, and the sound of the screen door guarantees Jake's intent to welcome his unknown quest.

Melanie exits the car and scrutinizes Jake from behind her dark sunglasses. His Levi's and flannel shirt are befitting a man who holds a car part in his hand. His face shows little signs of age, though it is difficult to make an accurate assessment because grease shields his cheeks and forehead. His charming smile fails to incite the same feelings it once did. And though his striking blue eyes gaze at her with open appreciation, she holds her emotional defenses high and refuses to let him affect her heart.

Melanie is older and wiser now, and everything about Jake Perry disgusts her. But she realizes the truth of their situation–she belongs to him. Though she'd been running from him for seven years, she is just as much bound to him now as she was when she said, "I do." The only difference is that now she no longer desires him.

I must be honest with you. At times, I find the Lord less than desirable. When he shrouds himself in ambiguity and requires that I respond to him in faith, I find myself increasingly frustrated with him. During times like these, there are no feelings of love and affection that arise within me. On the contrary, I often feel alone and forgotten. And worst of all, I feel like giving up on this relationship with my creator.

Sometimes it is God's distant behavior that drives me crazy but more often than not it's my own wandering heart that creates a rift

4. Adam Clarke, "Commentary on 1 Thessalonians 5," *The Adam Clarke Commentary*, 1832, http://www.studylight.org/com/acc/view.cgi?book=1th&chapter=5&verse=19#1Th5_19.

in our relationship. It doesn't have to be some horrible, illicit sin that separates me from God. Usually, the sin of apathy takes a much harder toll on my relationship with the Lord than high-profile sins such as lying, lust, and envy. Those sins are easily identifiable, and I'm able to recognize my folly instantly. But the sin of indifference toward God is subtle and insidious. It entertains me with other things (gods) while quietly stealing my affections away from the Savior. And before long, I've forsaken my first love.

In fact, over the last several months I fear that's what has occurred. You see, whenever I write, there is a closeness, an intimacy I share with the Lord. I am more dependent upon him when I write than I am at any other time in my life. But almost a year has passed since I penned my first study. And I'm ashamed to say, but my relationship with the Lord has suffered. I've not had to be as dependent upon him. I've not had to be as attuned to his Holy Spirit. And because I haven't had to be, somewhere along the way I decided not to be.

Sometimes I'm tracking with the Holy Spirit, attune to his guidance, submitted to his will. And at other times, I prefer the path of apathy. Disinterested in his direction, choosing to ignore him, opting instead to watch that shady movie or entertain myself with that off-colored joke. After hours, days, and weeks of continually choosing to disregard God's Spirit, my heart becomes hardened, and I no longer desire God. Though I still belong to him, my heart is no longer affected by him.

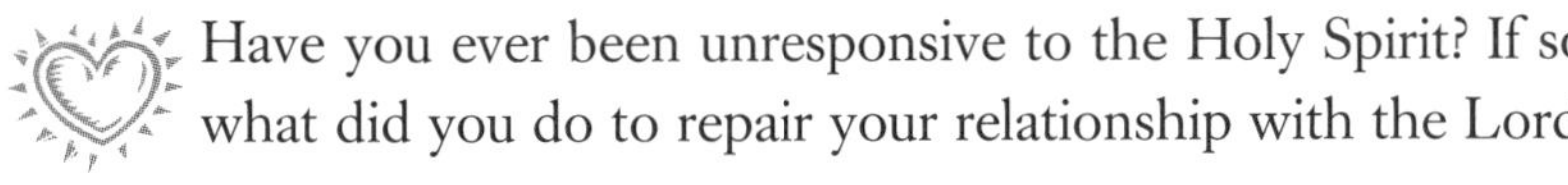

Have you ever been unresponsive to the Holy Spirit? If so, what did you do to repair your relationship with the Lord?

____

____

____

Staring at the striking blond before him, Jake notes the woman's appearance. The black leather boots she wears would do her little good at the county rodeo. Her dark blouse and expensive skirt are too trendy to have been purchased at the local Wal-Mart. And the sporty car she drives isn't engineered for country roads. No, this little lady isn't from around here. Or so Jake thinks.

Standing on his front porch, Jake watches as the stranger's perfectly manicured hand flies to her face, removing designer sunglasses. The removal of those shades reveals a pair of eyes he has never forgotten. Eyes he has seen for many years only in his dreams. And in that moment, Jake realizes he isn't dreaming. Those eyes are real, and they belong to his wife. She has finally returned home.

I have spent the last several weeks doing what the Lord told the Ephesians to do in Revelation 2:5. I've been remembering and repenting. I've remembered my past experiences with the Lord, how he always showed himself faithful, even when he seemed distant and required I follow him in faith. I've remembered the tender way his Holy Spirit would whisper his will into my heart, and even though I didn't want to obey, he encouraged me to do so. I've remembered the love he's allowed me to enjoy, both a love *from* him and a love *for* him. And it's in the remembering that I've been able to appreciate all I've lost.

Thankfully, these precious moments with the Lord are not lost for good. Because you see, along with remembering, I've been repenting too. I was wrong to allow God's Holy Spirit to become *quenched* in my life. I was wrong to ignore his protective hand of guidance. I was wrong to disregard his voice. I was wrong–so I've asked for God's forgiveness. And because I am his, covered by his son's blood and sealed by the Holy Spirit with his authenticity of ownership, I am forgiven. And once again, I am finally home.

Prayer–*Loving Lord, though I may not stray as far as some, I know when I am ignoring your Holy Spirit's guidance in my life. Thank you that your love provides me with your precious Holy Spirit. Please give me the grace I need to listen and obey your Spirit, for my life no longer belongs to me. It belongs solely to you. So thank you for never giving up on me. And thank you for giving me your precious Holy Spirit to guide me back home.*

Day 4: His Love Provides the Opportunity to Know Him

Read Ephesians 1:15–17.

Oh, Melanie has returned home alright, but after uttering her first words of contempt, Jake knows instantly her visit will be an unpleasant one. Gone is the fearless free spirit he married. The woman who glares at him now is cultured, refined, and incredibly snotty. Her condescending manner, haughty tone, and persistent demands for divorce prove she is most definitely not his Mel.

The verses we will study today form the first portion of Paul's prayer for the Ephesians. We will study the second portion of his prayer in Day 5, so for now, let's direct our focus to verses 15 through 17.

Read Ephesians 1:15–16 and fill in the blank below:

"For this reason, ever since I heard about your ________________ in the Lord Jesus and your love for all the saints, I have not stopped giving thanks for you, remembering you in my prayers."

Read Ephesians 1:17. Why did Paul ask God to give the Ephesians the Spirit of wisdom and revelation?

Jake understands her demands for divorce. Though he doesn't agree, he knows she is entitled to seek one. Seven years ago he withheld so much of himself from her. He hadn't shared everything because, heck, he didn't know there was so much of himself left to share. But, time has been a scrupulous teacher, and he no longer stands in ignorance of himself. He is a changed man with more to offer her now than he had before. He has a purpose in life. He has a successful career. He knows who he is; he only hopes she'll stay long enough to get to know the real Jake Perry.

Have you ever found yourself in a relationship with someone whom you really didn't know? If so, how did you get to know them?

The bar is crowded with rednecks downing beers and shooting pool. Their topic of conversation centers around old high school football games and a time when their beer bellies wouldn't have prevented them from running the winning touchdown. The scene is pathetic. Melanie longs for New York and Andrew. But she refuses to let Jake delay their divorce any longer, so she's followed him here. In the smoke-filled room, she encounters childhood friends and high school buddies, all of whom seem to hold Jake in high regard. As if he's made something of himself down at the tire factory. No, Jake Perry has nothing to offer Melanie Carmichael. She is certain of that. He is lazy and usually up to no good. She knows all about him. She made up her mind about Jake a long time ago. And she knows him well enough to know he'll never change.

According to Paul's commendation in verse 15, the Ephesians were exercising their faith. But though the Ephesians possessed a faith in the Lord, they still needed more. Faith in God is a necessary element for salvation, and it's essential for every Christian's continued walk with Christ, but God grants us more than faith. He gives us the opportunity to truly know him.

Paul knew that in order to maintain a healthy relationship with the Lord, the Ephesians would need to go beyond just believing in God for salvation. They'd need to take steps to truly know God.

Melanie doesn't know why she decided to stay in town. At this point, Jake had already given her what she wanted. Yet here she is at the fair, surrounded by Lurlynn's four children–a most unpleasant experience. Lurlynn doles out food to her little urchins then turns to Melanie and speaks with a French fry in her mouth. Her words shake Melanie to the core. Jake had come after her? How? Why? When? Lurlynn doesn't need much prodding, she willingly tells Melanie all she knows.

It had taken him a year to work up the nerve to pursue her. New York had both amazed and intimidated Jake. The allure of that big city and the fact that Melanie sought solace there convinced him he couldn't persuade her to return to him by offering her a mere apology; he'd have to offer her the world. So he'd spent the last six years trying to conquer it.

The Greek word translated "know" in verse 17 is *epignosis,* meaning "knowledge that is true, accurate, thorough, full knowledge."[5] Paul's prayer for the Ephesians is that they have a true, accurate knowledge of the God they served. Not a clouded, mystic view of him or an opinion based upon assumptions, but a concise under-

5. Wuest, 52.

standing of his nature and character, of his likes and dislikes, of his sources of joy and pleasure.

Though Melanie thought she knew her estranged husband, she was wrong. She hadn't seen him in years, and yet she based her opinion of him on assumptions she'd made seven years ago. She had no knowledge of the man he was now. But that didn't stop her from drawing her own conclusions and making her own suppositions. The truth was not her goal, and the acquisition of accurate information was not her intent. Therefore the reality of the matter was that Melanie thought she knew Jake, when in essence, she didn't know him at all.

"The Christian life could be described as getting to know God better every day."[6]

My dear friend, don't make the same mistake Melanie makes in this film story. Don't assume you know everything there is to know about the God we serve. There is so much of him to discover. And though it will take all of eternity for us to ascertain the various qualities and characteristics of our Lord, we must never deny ourselves the opportunity to get to know him more.

Think about your relationship with the Lord. What do you know about God?

____

____

____

____

I know that unlike Jake, who merely *attempted* to conquer the world, my God *did* conquer the world. Wow! What a hero! I know he's a great safe-haven when I've suffered rejection and shame. But

6. William Barclay, *The Letters to the Galatians and Ephesians* (Philadelphia: The Westminster Press, 1958), 105.

he's also a mighty fortress when I've tried to get him to alter his plans to accommodate mine. I know he's quite fond of my obedience, but rather dislikes my vain attempts to control my life. I know he likes faith, my faith, especially when it's exercised under the most strenuous of circumstances.

I know he loves people–even one's I'm not quite fond of. And he has quite a sense of humor, because he allows me to encounter these difficult people on a regular basis. Also, I know he has little regard for time–especially when I'm waiting for something. He's available day or night and for some reason, he seems to think I am as well, because he often awakens me in the night–just to spend time with me.

I know he has thick skin, because I've repeatedly questioned his ways (in a somewhat condescending tone), and he's always listened to me vent and then sent me on my way. I know he's not afraid to make me mad and he's even less fearful of my discomfort. I know he's loving and gentle when the tears of sorrow and confusion roll down my cheeks. But he's firm and resolute when I'm in need of discipline.

But most of all, perhaps, I know that he loves for me to love him. Sometimes I'll be going about my daily tasks, completely absorbed in my grocery shopping or my cleaning and all of a sudden he'll squeeze my heart, generating within me such a love for him. It's a deep love. A love I can't produce on my own, so he gives it to me–by way of his Spirit. And this love he gives creates in me a desire to know him more. My prayer is that he will give you the same love and the same insatiable desire to know him more.

Prayer–*Precious Father, thank you that your love provides me the opportunity to know you. And while I'll never know every facet of your character during my stay on earth, I am so grateful you disclose portions of yourself to me. May you do the same for all your children and may you give each of us an insatiable desire to know you more.*

Day 5: His Love Provides Power

Read Ephesians 1:18–23.

They say lightning never strikes twice in the same place. But they're wrong. Reports indicate the Empire State Building is struck an average of a hundred times a year. Its immense size continually attracts nature's wrath, sustaining bolts of lightning that are 50,000 degrees Fahrenheit and five times hotter than the sun.[7] But the heat of the bolt is not the only thing the Empire State Building must endure. The proud structure must sustain the power of the bolt. One lightning strike contains several hundred million volts of electrical current. If this power were ever harnessed, it could provide enough electricity for ten million homes–for one month.[8]

The rain beats down on Jake as he hammers his lightning rods into the beach. He hopes to channel the power of the lightning bolt and direct it toward the damp sand, causing the formation of a fulgurite. The glass-like structure formed by the fusion of sand has made him a successful businessman and has proven that, to some degree, man can harness the power of lightning. But all the power in the world cannot give him what he truly wants.

Paul's prayer continues in Ephesians 1:18–19. According to these verses, what three things does Paul want the Ephesians to know?

7. Wikipedia: The Free Encyclopedia. "Lightning," http://en.wikipedia.org/wiki/Lightning#_ref-ucar_0.
8. Duquesne Light. "The Power of Lightning," http://pruc.duquesnelight.com/PowerOutages/UsefulTips/PowerLightning.cfm.

Yesterday we discussed Paul's prayer for the Ephesians to know God. Today we'll talk about Paul's desire for the Ephesians to know all that God offers. In verse 18, Paul expresses his desire for the Ephesians to know the hope of their calling, or rather, the hope to which God has called them. Paul wants them to fully acknowledge the benefit of their salvation and the hope it offers. Because of God's salvation, they are granted the hope of eternal life.

How do you feel about eternity? Do you look at it with hope and expectation, or dread and fear?

____

____

____

Read 1 Thessalonians 4:14–17 and finish the statement found in verse 17.

"And so we will be with the Lord ______________."

Regardless of our feelings about eternity, God is eagerly anticipating a future spent with us. Paul supports this belief in Ephesians 1:18 by praying that the Ephesians know the riches of God's inheritance in the saints. According to scholars, this statement is not in reference to the saints' inheritance, it's in reference to God's inheritance.

We are what God has to look forward to throughout all eternity. We are his inheritance, and he considers himself rich because he has us.

Read Deuteronomy 32:9 and fill in the blank below.

"The Lord's portion is his ________________."

In this verse, the word "portion" suggests an award. We are God's inheritance. We are his portion. We are his award. What a tender way to view our relationship with the Lord. But Paul goes on to display another aspect of all God has to offer. First there is the hope of our calling, then the riches of his inheritance in the saints, and finally, there is his incomparably great power for us who believe.

Paul compares this great power to the power God exerted in Christ's life. Read Ephesians 1:19–23 and describe the things God did in Christ's life to display his power.

God's power is greater than any lightning bolt, for that matter, any source of electrical current. God's power doesn't just strike proud structures with a hundred million volts of electricity; it raises people from the dead. God's power raised Christ from the dead and in so doing, reveals God's power over death. But God's power doesn't stop there. God shows his supremacy over all authority and dominion by placing all things under Christ's feet. He shows his power over time by placing Christ at the helm of authority for all eternity. With these acts of preeminence, it's safe to say we serve an all-powerful God. And it's encouraging to know that God's power is at work on our behalf. But there is one area in which God stays his all-powerful hand.

Thunder sounds in the distance, announcing the arrival of lightning. And yet Jake is unfazed by the force of nature. His mind is elsewhere, turned toward thoughts of the heart and struck by the awareness of his helpless situation.

Mel is now free. He no longer holds any power over her. He had relinquished his claim on her life, when he signed those papers. He in essence had liberated her. He'd signed the papers, and she was now free from her obligation of him. She was free to choose another. He'd loved her enough to set her free. He'd loved her enough to give her the choice of whom to love. And she hadn't chosen him.

What does Joshua tell the Israelites in Joshua 24:15?

____

____

____

This week, we've discussed all the things God's love provides. In Day 1, we discussed how God's love provides acceptance. In Day 2, we talked about how God's love provides grace. In Day 3, we learned that God's love provides us with the Holy Spirit. Day 4 enlightened us to the fact that God's love provides us the opportunity to know God. And finally, in Day 5, we have been learning that our all-powerful God gives us a love that provides power.

But the power God's love provides is not the power for us to rule the world–he's doing a fine job without our assistance. What his love provides us is the power to reject the ruler of the world. We have the power to choose whether we love him or reject him. The power is ours. He's given us everything we need to be in right relationship with him and to maintain a healthy relationship with him. But he's also given us the power to reject that relationship.

The borrowed pen hovers over the legal document. Jake's signature had already been applied, but the line above her name remains empty. How could Melanie have made such a critical oversight? One stroke of the pen, and it would all be over. She would be free. This is what she wanted, right? This is what she needed to do. Her destiny awaits her at the end of the aisle and yet somehow, she longs for the man from her past. The man who had relinquished his claim on her life. The man who had made himself vulnerable to her. The man who had freed her from her obligation and now gave her the power to love him or reject him. She longed for Jake.

Dear friend, our all-powerful God has made himself vulnerable to mankind by giving us the choice to love him or reject him. He's given us the power to decide. He doesn't have to. He has control of all authority and dominion, over the future and the past, over life and death. Surely a God with such displays of power could have easily taken our wayward hearts and enforced his control. But instead, he's chosen not to. He's given us the power to decide. That fact alone causes me to love him all the more.

In *Sweet Home Alabama* how did you feel after you watched Melanie make her decision about Jake? How do you think God feels when we decide to love him?

Prayer–*Mighty God, thank you for using your power to reclaim your son from the vise-grip of death. Thank you for demonstrating your power by placing Christ above all rule, authority and dominion, both in this age and in the age to come. Thank you that your power knows no bounds, save the ones you place upon it. And for some reason, you placed boundaries for yourself around the perimeter of my heart. You could have enforced my love, and yet you didn't. You gave me the power to decide. Just knowing that makes me love you all the more. So may it be known both in this age and in the age to come that now and forever, I choose to love you in return.*

HIS LOVE UNIFIES

Ephesians 2

VOW: "His purpose was to create in himself one new man out of the two, thus making peace, and in this one body to reconcile both of them to God . . ."	**Ephesians 2:15–16**

Day 1: United in Sin

Read Ephesians 2:1–3.

As the daughter of acting legend, John Barrymore, Drew Barrymore made her acting debut early in life. At eleven months of age she starred in a dog food commercial and continued to do small acting jobs throughout her preschool years. In 1982, when Barrymore was just six years old, she landed the role of Gertie in Steven Spielberg's movie, *ET*. Her performance left audiences in a quandary, unsure of whom to love most, the big-hearted alien with a weakness for Reese's pieces, or the adorable little Gertie, whose pig tails and pixy smile made her simply irresistible.

As a result of *ET*'s success, Barrymore became an international star. But the pressures of fame proved too difficult for Barrymore, whose preteen years were marred by substance abuse and addiction. She discovered alcohol and cigarettes at the age of nine while partying with her mother, Jaid, in Hollywood's trendiest clubs. By age ten the numbing effect of alcohol had increased her urge for chemical substances, so she sought solace in marijuana. By age twelve, she had moved on to cocaine and was by all accounts, an addict.

Read Ephesians 2:1–2.

Who is Paul addressing in this passage?

____

____

How does he describe them in verse 1?

____

____

____

What does he say they were doing in verse 2?

____

____

____

By the age of fourteen, Barrymore had been an addict, been to rehab, and been discarded by Hollywood. Of that time in her life, Barrymore says, "I was a complete has-been by the time I was 14. Isn't that an achievement?"[1]

1. Jon Wilde, "Getaway Girl," *The Mail on Sunday*, February 11, 2007.

It's hard for me to identify with Barrymore's woes. I've never achieved the status of "has-been," mainly because that title would have required me to actually "have been somebody" of fame at some point in my life. So I'm disqualified from that label. I've never been in a movie. In fact, I've never been to Hollywood and certainly not to one of Hollywood's trendiest clubs. I've never smoked pot. I've never tried cocaine. And I've never been in rehab.

In Ephesians 2:3, Paul changes his pronouns. No longer is he solely recounting the Ephesians' sins, now he includes himself (and his companions) in this description of debauchery. What does he say about the way he (and others) once lived?

Ephesians 2 is about unity. And though I bear no striking similarities to the famed Drew Barrymore, there is one thing that unites us–sin. My transgressions may not be nearly as taboo in nature, but I too have gratified the cravings of this sinful nature, following its selfish desires and lustful thoughts.

Have you? Are you like Drew and me?

Sin linked Paul to the church at Ephesus. Though Paul's past sins included transgressions made on behalf of the Jewish faith, the Ephesians' sins were probably more worldly in nature, leaning toward idolatry and sorcery due to the city in which they lived. But no matter the type of sin, the tendency toward sin was evident in all.

Reread Ephesians 2:3 and fill in the blank.

"Like the rest, we were by nature objects of ______________."

Because our Creator is a holy God, *any* offense against his law and righteousness merits his wrath. Therefore, any wrongdoing on our part makes us deserving of his wrath. We have all violated at least one of his Ten Commandments to some degree or another. We've all made mistakes; we've all indulged this sinful nature. Romans 3:23 says, "for all have sinned and fall short of the glory of God."

Have you ever compared your sins to others? If so, you were left feeling either one of two ways: shameful or prideful. Which did you feel? Explain your answer.

____

____

____

____

Perhaps, compared to Drew Barrymore, I have led a rather saintly life. One might even make the assumption that my sins pale in comparison to hers. But with God, there is no qualitative sin scale. There's no ranking for sins. The sin of pride is just as depraved in God's eyes as the sin of overindulgence or the sin of excess. No sin is worse than any other. Certain sins may carry greater repercussions here on earth, but in God's eyes, sin is sin. And by God's standard, my transgressions are just as vile as the sins of others.

It's a humbling thought to realize that sin unites us. But it does. We are united with the worst of sinners because we too have committed crimes against God's law. We're all united in our sin, and we're all united in our need for a Savior.

Prayer—*Lord, we are all sinners saved by grace. Thank you that the realization of that one fact makes your gift of salvation all the more precious.*

Day 2: "Little Girl Lost" United with Christ

Read Ephesians 2:4–10.

In 1989, the drugs no longer assuaged the feelings of loneliness and insecurity. So for Drew Barrymore, the only way of escape was suicide. But after a failed attempt, the thirteen-year-old opted for rehab and a year later released her autobiography, *Little Girl Lost*, chronicling her short but turbulent life.

Read Ephesians 2:4–5.

What did God do for us in verse 5?

According to verse 4, why did he do it?

Like Barrymore, we were all little girls lost, in need of rescue, caught in sin and dead in our transgressions. Yet in the midst of our fallen state, God united us with his son and gave us life. I like the way

The Message Bible puts it, "It's a wonder God didn't lose his temper and do away with the whole lot of us. Instead, immense in mercy and with an incredible love, he embraced us. He took our sin-dead lives and made us alive in Christ."

Can't you just picture the God of the universe taking a filthy urchin and enfolding her within the safety of his embrace? And then passing her from his arms, to the arms of his son? What an unusual act for a king. Only a kind and loving king could offer such mercy and grace. And our king does just that. But in addition to his love and affection, he gives us yet another treasure–he gives us life. Not just an eternal existence in solitude, but everlasting life with his son by our side.

Read Ephesians 2:6–7. What did God do for us in verse 6?

____

____

____

Hollywood's "little girl lost" kept a low profile for the remainder of her teen years. She completed rehab and remained sober despite her floundering acting career. But in 1998, Drew Barrymore made a surprising comeback in the low-budget, blockbuster film, *The Wedding Singer.* Her performance in the romantic comedy gave audiences the opportunity to see a sweet and vulnerable Drew on the big screen, thus creating a demand for Drew in a host of other love stories. One such love story was the film *Ever After,* starring Barrymore opposite Scottish actor, Dougray Scott.

In this version of the Brothers Grimm's fairy tale, the little Cinder girl catches the eye of the handsome prince. And he longs to make her his bride–to rescue her from her lowly state, to usher her into his kingdom and seat her upon his throne. It may seem like a cheesy, romantic fairy tale, but it's exactly what the Lord did for you.

How do you feel knowing you are God's modern-day Cinderella?

____

____

____

____

____

Reread Ephesians 2:7, why did God do this for you?

____

____

____

The story of Cinderella has been passed down for hundreds of years. The German "Brothers Grimm" recorded their version in the nineteenth century, while the French version of Cinderella was written in 1634. The Chinese version was penned in AD 860, and the earliest known version of Cinderella is the Greco-Egyptian version dating back to the first century BC. Though the details of the story vary, the essence of the story remains the same. The destitute slave girl is rescued by the handsome prince. He claims her as his own and offers her a new life with him.

I believe the story of Cinderella has endured for thousands of years because it personifies the story of Christ's love for his bride. Cinderella is our story, not written by Brothers Grimm, but written by God. Penned by the hand of the creator and recorded for all the world to read. So that throughout the ages, the author of our love story might receive the praise and the glory and that all might live happily ever after.

Prayer–*Lord, thank you for what you have done for me. Thank you for uniting me with your son and for giving me a new life with him. May our love story be inscribed upon the pages of my heart for all the world to read.*

Day 3: United with God's Family

Read Ephesians 2:11–13.

Life had not been easy for little Danielle De Barbarac, but today is not a day to reminisce about past woes. Today she will see her father. And he will give her a family–a mother and siblings of her very own.

Movie Mania

To better understand this study of Ephesians 2, watch *Ever After* and consider the following questions:

- Why did Danielle try so hard to please her stepmother?
- Did her stepmother treat Danielle like family?

Danielle's excitement soon turns to sorrow. First she endures the death of her beloved father. And thereafter she daily endures the rejection of her stepmother. Though Danielle continually hopes to please the baroness and somehow earn her acceptance, it seems as though all of Danielle's efforts are for naught. She is the outsider, and her stepmother and stepsisters will never let her in.

Paul's letter to the Ephesians provides hope for every Gentile with aspirations of following the Jewish Messiah. In the second chapter of Ephesians, Paul specifically addresses this group of struggling Gentiles trying to access the impenetrable walls of the Jewish faith. A faith that once shunned them would now be made available to them through the blood of Christ.

According to Ephesians 2:11, what were the Gentiles called?

In Genesis 17, God instructed Abraham to undergo circumcision as a sign of the covenant made between himself and Abraham. All of Abraham's descendants (the Jews) were also to undergo circumcision as a reminder of that covenant. As a result, two groups existed among the early church–the uncircumcised Gentiles and the circumcised Jews.

In Ephesians 2:12, Paul lists five aspects of the former state in which the Gentiles lived. What were they?

Not only were the Gentiles considered the "uncircumcised," but they were also formerly in a state of separation from Christ. They were excluded from citizenship in Israel. They were foreigners to the covenants of the promise. They were without hope. And they were without God in the world.

Paul uses these five aspects of the Gentiles' former state as reminders of the hopelessness from which they came. According to Old Testament law, they had no right to share in the promises given to the Jews.

According to your own ethnic descent, are you a Jew or a Gentile?

What does Ephesians 2:13 say God did for the Gentiles?

"Blessed are those you choose and bring near to live in your courts!" Psalm 65:4

Not many of us are descendants of the Jewish race, so in some ways, we too share in the hopeless state of the early Christian Gentiles. But thankfully, God did for us what we could not do for ourselves. He brought us near through the blood of Christ. He unified us with his chosen people, the Jews, and he gave us an opportunity to share in his inheritance.

Have you ever been given entrance into a group in which you really did not belong? If so, cite your experience and how it made you feel.

Prayer—*Lord, not only did you accept me as your child, but you made a way for your chosen people, the Jews to accept me as well. Thank you for your grace toward me.*

Day 4: Experiencing Unity

Read Ephesians 2:14–18.

The beautiful dress does nothing to change Danielle's station in life. She is, and forever will be, a peasant and no amount of fabric can alter that fact. But today, she plays the part of a noblewoman. Her flowing gown, haughty air, and bulging purse are all part of the persona. Hopefully it will be enough to convince the guards she is a courtier. If so, then she'll be granted access to court, and Maurice will soon be free.

In Day 3, we discussed the divisions that existed among Jews and Gentiles. In the verses we will study today, Paul gives us some insight as to how Christ destroyed those divisions.

According to Ephesians 2:14, what did Christ destroy?

____

____

____

Throughout history, there have been three temples for Jewish worship. All built in Jerusalem on Mt. Moriah, these three temples existed during different periods in Jewish history. Solomon's Temple, built by King Solomon around 950 BC, was said to be one of the Seven Wonders of the Ancient World. However, it was destroyed in 586 BC when the Babylonians captured Jerusalem.

Around 536 BC, the Jews were allowed to return to Jerusalem. Under the direction of their appointed governor, Zerubbabel, they began rebuilding the temple. This temple, which is referred to as Zerubbabel's Temple, was rebuilt during the decades between 530 and 500 BC.

During the New Testament, while the Romans ruled Jerusalem, King Herod endeavored to make God's temple one of the most beautiful buildings in history. So in 47 BC, he began a four-decade building project to expand Zerubbabel's Temple. According to famed historian Josephus, King Herod actually doubled the size of the Temple Mount by erecting new walls. One such wall that surrounded the outer perimeter of the Temple was called the *soreg*. And it formed the barrier between the Gentile's Court and the rest of the temple.

The twenty gold francs jingle in her purse as the smell of the soldiers' horses accompany Danielle on her walk to the castle. The tall formidable walls of the king's lair are intimidating to a young servant girl. But Maurice's life is at stake, so with head held high, she approaches the guards. Just beyond the burly men lies her destination–the courtyard where the courtiers gather. Danielle can see them, men and women of title, dressed in fine array, whose noble birth grants them access to the king's presence.

According to Jewish law, the Gentiles could never be granted access to the Lord's presence, nor could they enter his temple. They might stand outside the perimeter in the Gentile's Court; however, any entrance into the temple beyond that point was limited to Jews alone. Josephus wrote that the *soreg*, or barrier wall, separating the Gentile's Court from the rest of the temple, had an inscribed warning "which forbade any foreigner to go in under pain of death."[2] These warnings were posted intermittently along the barrier wall proving that physical, social, and spiritual divisions existed between the Jews and Gentiles.

2. Josephus, *Antiquities of the Jews*, 15:11:5.

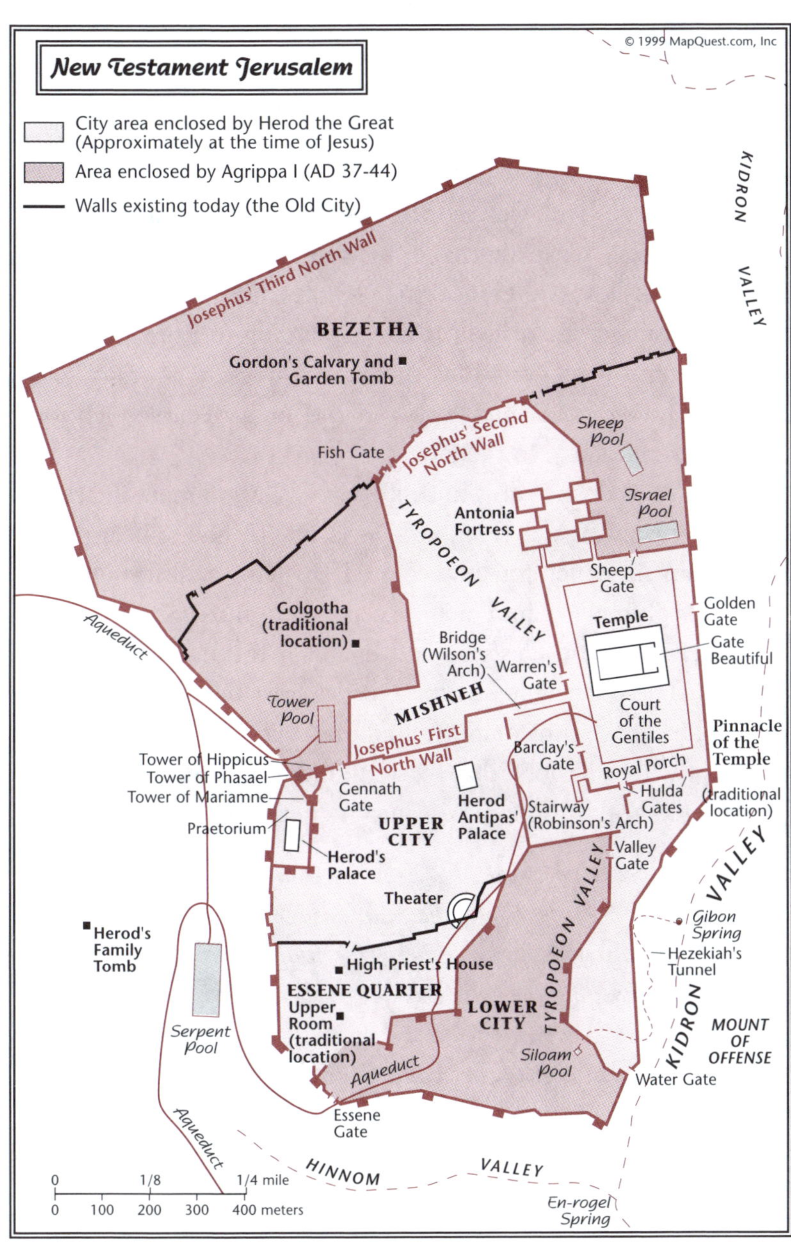
New Testament Jerusalem
© 1999 MapQuest.com, Inc
City area enclosed by Herod the Great (Approximately at the time of Jesus)
Area enclosed by Agrippa I (AD 37-44)
Walls existing today (the Old City)
Josephus' Third North Wall
BEZETHA
Gordon's Calvary and Garden Tomb
KIDRON VALLEY
Fish Gate
Josephus' Second North Wall
Sheep Pool
Israel Pool
Antonia Fortress
TYROPOEON VALLEY
Sheep Gate
Golden Gate
Temple
Gate Beautiful
Golgotha (traditional location)
Aqueduct
Bridge (Wilson's Arch)
Warren's Gate
MISHNEH
Tower Pool
Court of the Gentiles
Pinnacle of the Temple (traditional location)
Josephus' First North Wall
Barclay's Gate
Royal Porch
Tower of Hippicus
Tower of Phasael
Tower of Mariamne
Gennath Gate
Hulda Gates
Praetorium
UPPER CITY
Herod Antipas' Palace
Stairway (Robinson's Arch)
Herod's Palace
Valley Gate
VALLEY
Theater
Gibon Spring
Hezekiah's Tunnel
Herod's Family Tomb
High Priest's House
ESSENE QUARTER
Upper Room (traditional location)
LOWER CITY
KIDRON
MOUNT OF OFFENSE
Serpent Pool
Siloam Pool
Aqueduct
Water Gate
Essene Gate
Aqueduct
HINNOM VALLEY
0 1/8 1/4 mile
0 100 200 300 400 meters
En-rogel Spring

Read the first portion of Ephesians 2:15. How did Christ destroy the dividing wall?

The dividing wall was erected because the Jews were under the Law of Moses. "The law made a definite distinction between the Jews and Gentiles . . . (because) the Gentiles did not obey these laws; therefore they were unclean."[3] Also, according to Romans 3:20, the law made the Jews conscious of sin. As a result, hostility existed between the sin-conscious Jews and the sinful Gentiles who were not held accountable to the law.

In order to destroy this hostility, Christ had to meet the requirements of the law, which bound the Jews, and he had to bear the punishment for sin which the law required. By living a perfect life, Christ met the righteous requirements of the law, thus freeing the Jews from their legalistic lifestyles and enabling the union of Jews and Gentiles. Then, by dying on the cross, Christ bore the punishment for mankind's sin, thus uniting sinful man with God. His actions did away with the divisions that existed among the Jews and Gentiles and granted both groups access into the presence of the king.

Though she speaks no words, Danielle is certain the sound of her racing pulse will draw the attention of the guards. To compensate for her fears, she lifts her chin an inch higher and feigns indifference as she passes the brawny men guarding the gate. But her resolve almost crumples when she hears the voice of one of the soldiers. His guttural tone speaks of authority and power, but his words bring Danielle reassurance as he ushers her into court with the command that others make way for the lady. For the first time in her life, she makes it past the dividing wall and is granted access into the courtyard of the king.

3. Warren Wiersbe, *Be Rich* (Colorado Springs: Cook Communications, 2004), 58.

The Jews in Ephesus were most likely raised under a sin-conscious law that separated them from their Gentile brothers in the faith. Being raised with standards of righteousness can be a good thing, but when we allow that righteous law to separate us from others who long to enter the Lord's presence, then we too build dividing walls.

What are some dividing walls that can be built between Christians?

Many denominations have invoked standards of holiness such as abstaining from alcohol or wearing certain types of clothing. Some people dictate righteousness by one's doctrinal beliefs or church affiliation. Others determine virtue by one's tithe record or giving statement. All of these things have the propensity to be dividing walls between Christians–walls that were never meant to be built between brothers and sisters of the faith.

Read Ephesians 2:15–16. What was Christ's purpose?

Read Ephesians 2:17–18. As a result of Christ's work, who do we now have access to?

Christ's purpose can be summed up in one word, "unity"–unity with man and unity with God. As a result of Christ's finished work on the cross, we not only have access to our brothers and sisters in Christ, we also have access to God.

Do you feel completely unified with your brothers and sisters in Christ, or are there some dividing walls that are difficult to break down? If so, what are they?

Prayer–*Lord, I don't want to miss out on the unity you provide through Christ. I don't want to miss out on unity with you or with my brothers and sisters in the faith. So please, Lord, show me dividing walls that may be separating me from true unity with you and with others.*

Day 5: "Unity That Offers Not Just Acceptance, but Equality"

Read Ephesians 2:19–22.

Entrance into the courtyard was all Danielle had hoped to gain. An audience with the prince had not been one of her desires. Nonetheless, here she is, stating her claim and quoting Utopia *in an attempt to rescue Maurice. What she wouldn't do for that dear man who had served her father's household so faithfully! Now she only hopes her bravado will be enough to save him.*

In Ephesians 2:19–20, Paul speaks directly to the Gentiles. What does he tell them in verse 19?

____

____

____

Freedom makes Maurice rather exuberant in his displays of affection. He embraces Danielle with sincere gratitude, but his informal manner places them in danger of discovery. Danielle nervously searches the crowd of spectators, fearing one of them might realize she is not who she claims to be. But no one seems suspicious of her or her servant. So maintaining an air of restraint, Danielle grabs the old man by the arms and instructs him to prepare the horses for their departure.

A sigh of relief escapes Danielle's lips as she completes the customary curtsy before the prince and begins to walk toward the gate. Only a few more steps and she will be free of this farce. Surely she is a fool for such impetuous actions. Though she had once been heir to her father's household, commanding respect and honor from her father's servants, now she is nothing more than a servant herself. The arrival of the baroness had instigated that demotion. But servitude has not robbed Danielle of her pride or her love for her own. She loves Maurice and the others, for they are more than servants; they are family.

The Greek word translated "alien" in verse 19 is *paroikos* meaning "a stranger who lives in a place without the right of citizenship."[4] Though Maurice had lived in Danielle's home for years, he was not truly a member of the household. He had no rights of citizenship, no

4. James Strong, *Strong's Exhaustive Concordance of the Bible*, http://www.studylight.org/isb/view.cgi?number=3941.

privileges granted next of kin. The baroness had made sure of that. But in Danielle's heart, he was a member of the family.

Before the coming of Christ, the Gentiles were considered second rate. They may have lived among the Jews, even worshiped in the outer courts of their temple, but they were strangers among God's people. They were outsiders, denied access into the family of God.

Read Galatians 4:4–7 and fill in the blank below:

"So you are no longer a ________________, but a ___________."

When God opened his heart to the Gentiles, he not only granted them acceptance, he granted them equality. He gave them the same status he offered the Jews. He made them sons, and he united them with his most precious possession–his people.

God had a purpose for uniting the Jews and the Gentiles. According to Ephesians 2:21–22, what was that purpose?

____

____

____

What did God say in 2 Corinthians 6:16?

____

____

God has always desired to be near his people. He was not content to remain afar off, confined to a temple made by human hands. He deserved better. He deserved to reside within temples that he himself fashioned and created from the dust of the earth. He deserved to live within these temples where hearts beat for him. But prior to his son's sacrifice on the cross, God could not enter the hearts of mankind because of the sin that existed there. When Christ came to earth and gave himself up to be crucified, his sacrifice covered our sins and made us holy and blameless in God's sight. And now we have access to the Father by his Spirit, because his Spirit lives in us.

Reread Ephesians 2:21 and fill in the blanks.

"In Him the whole building is ____________ ____________ and rises to become a holy temple in the Lord."

According to Ephesians 2:22, God's Spirit lives in each of us individually. But his presence also dwells within the body of Christ as a whole (Christ's church), so that every believer is essential for the overall construction of a holy temple in the Lord.

God took a group of sinful outsiders and united them with his people. He took second-class citizens, slaves rather, and made them sons. God gave the Gentiles a place in his new society. No longer would they be foreigners or aliens, denied entrance into the temple. Now they, together with the Jewish Christians, would *be* the temple collectively, or the church.

Sometimes in Christian circles, it's easy to categorize people as good, better, and best or necessary and unnecessary. But in God's society, we are all equal. One is not better than the other; the Jew is not greater than the Gentile; the talented is not above the seemingly untalented; the spiritually mature mentor is not above the new Christian. All are needed for the work of the gospel. All enjoy the benefits of the Holy Spirit housed within them and all are essential to the building project of God's overall holy temple.

How do you think the Gentile Christians felt when they read Ephesians 2:19–22? Do you think they truly believed they were equal to the Jews? Do you suppose they saw themselves as essential to the building of God's holy temple?

____

Have you ever been tempted to question your worth in the body of Christ? Have you ever looked around at others who were doing great things for God and felt seemingly inadequate and unnecessary?

If so, write out how you feel now after reading Ephesians 2:19–22.

Prayer–*Lord, thank you that I need my brothers and sisters in Christ. Thank you that I need them and they need me. I am an essential part of your building project and I yield my life to you. Unite me with all those who belong to you, make us your sons, equal in your eyes. And make us into your holy temple.*

HIS LOVE REVEALS

Ephesians 3

VOW: "And I pray that you, being rooted and established in love, may have power, together with all the saints . . . to know this love that surpasses knowledge."	Ephesians 3:17–19

Day 1: God's Love Revealed through Suffering

Read Ephesians 3:1.

The streets of New York are crowded with people, but Alex Hitchens (a.k.a. Hitch) knows them. Not their names, but their hearts' desires. He knows because he studies people. Actually, he studies relationships. And his research has given him some basic principles about this mysterious thing called love.

Movie Mania

To better understand this study of Ephesians 3, watch *Hitch* and consider the following questions:

- What function does Alex Hitchens (a.k.a. "Hitch") serve in the relationship between Albert Brennaman and Allegra Cole?
- Does Hitch believe in the product he is selling? Does he believe in great love, and does he allow himself to experience it?

Basic Principle:

No one ever wakes up and says, "Gee, I hope the God of the universe just completely ignores me today."

Now, they may say, "I'm not really into God" or "I'm not ready for a spiritual commitment right now." Or my personal favorite: "I'm really into my religion, and I don't have time for a relationship with God."

The Jews of the first century used that line a lot. But Paul wasn't a date doctor for the Jews. He was God's date doctor for the Gentiles. Whenever the Gentiles found out about God's interest in them, their pat answer was probably, "Gee, I didn't know God was even interested in me." Oh, he was interested alright. He was definitely interested. In fact, he still is interested. And Paul's life is proof of that.

Read Acts 9:15–16 and write what Christ told Ananias about Paul. (Pay close attention to the lovely prophecy given in verse 16.)

Paul should have known then that life would be rough, but I bet he had no idea what was in store for him.

Catch a glimpse of Paul's "sufferings" in 2 Corinthians 11:23–27. If these things had happened to you, what would you consider to be the worst, most painful trial?

I don't know if Paul had a "worst" physical trial. I'm sure that after a while, the pain just all seemed to blend together–although I'm certain he could have lived without the stoning. That experience really put him between a rock and a hard place, if you know what I mean.

But I wonder if the physical pain paled in comparison to the constant rejection he received. Rejection and injustice, those seemed to be the hallmarks of his ministerial career.

Read Ephesians 3:1.

How does Paul describe himself in this passage?

For whose sake does he suffer?

Paul was a missionary to the Gentiles. Therefore he had the difficult task of informing the Gentiles of Christ's intent to make them a part of his body and thereby make them his bride. This heavenly assignment garnered Paul a great deal of reproach from his fellow Jews.

At one time, Paul lived under the favor of the Jewish society in which he was born. But when he wrote Ephesians, he did so as a prisoner in Rome, confined to house arrest because of accusations from the Jews that he had transgressed the Law and defiled the temple.

Read Acts 21:17–29. According to the Jews' accusations in verse 28, what was the reason for Paul's imprisonment?

The four men referred to in this passage were Jews who had taken a Nazarite vow that rendered them "set apart" for the Lord for a specified season. By aligning himself with these men, Paul was hoping that the Jews would see that he followed the Law of Moses and was indeed not instructing Jews to forsake the Jewish faith.

In Week 2, we studied the *soreg,* or barrier wall, that divided the Gentile's Court from the outer perimeter of the temple. The *soreg* denied Gentiles entrance into the temple, and it was this barrier wall that was crossed by Paul and his four Jewish companions. But because Paul was suspected by the Jews of being a Gentile sympathizer, these men were mistaken for Gentiles, thus giving the angry Jews reason to accuse Paul of bringing Gentiles into the temple.

It was this occurrence that rendered Paul a prisoner at the time he wrote this letter to the Ephesians. In fact, at this point in time, he had been a prisoner for close to three years, and he was still awaiting a final verdict from the emperor of Rome.

Write Paul's words to the Gentiles in Ephesians 3:13.

____

____

____

The Gentile Ephesians, hearing of Paul's sufferings on their behalf may have been tempted to lose heart and succumb to discouragement over Paul's plight. But Paul wanted them to view his sufferings as evidence of God's great love for them.

Paul wanted the Gentiles in Ephesus to know of his trials. He wanted them to know of his imprisonment on their behalf. Not because he wanted them to feel guilty, but because he wanted them to grasp the depth of God's love for them.

Read Isaiah 43:4. What does God promise to do for those he loves?

____

____

____

Paul knew he was loved by God. In fact, his life was rooted and grounded in God's love. But there was a whole world of Gentiles who were ignorant of God's love for them. So Paul was given the high and holy calling of revealing God's love to them. He didn't just reveal God's love through words. He revealed it through his sufferings. He revealed it through his life. And in the end, he revealed it through his death.

The Gentiles were precious and honored in God's sight. He loved them dearly, and they needed to know the full extent of God's love.

As a Gentile, how do you see God's love for you reflected in the life and sufferings of Paul?

Prayer—*Lord, when I hear of Paul's sufferings, I often put myself in his shoes, and wonder what I would have done in his situation. But that's not what you're asking of me is it? Today, in these verses, you're asking me to put myself in the Gentiles' shoes—to feel what they felt. For when I do that, your great love becomes evident to me. You didn't let anything stop you, did you Lord? Your love letter to me was delivered through the hands of suffering saints who had grasped your great love for them and felt duty bound to pass that love on to others. Thank you Father for making me a recipient of that love. I receive it, Lord. I receive it!*

Day 2: God's Love Revealed in Spite of Rejection

Read Ephesians 3:2–6.

Basic Principle:

No one ever wakes up and says, "Gee, I've been rejected before, I think I'd like to experience that pain all over again."

Now they may say, "I've been rejected before and it stinks!" Or "I've been rejected, and I've just learned to live with it." Or my personal favorite, "I've been rejected before, and I've made sure it will never happen again."

I've been a proponent of the latter statement. Although it took me a few heartaches before I was willing to make that disclaimer. My first rejection occurred at the hands of my first boyfriend in the seventh grade. He dumped me for my best friend, whose name was Harmony. How ironic is that?

My second and perhaps most painful rejection came in college. It occurred when this guy I was crazy about dumped me for his ex-girlfriend, and then decided to marry her four months later–on my birthday. If that's not adding insult to injury, I don't know what is!

Cressida Baylor–the name still invoked a sharp pain in Hitch's heart. When he first met her he was just a foolish college boy, naïve to the ways of women. But Cressida had given him his first education. Why had he let his guard down? Why had he loved her so freely? And why had he, the great Date Doctor of New York City, ever allowed her the opportunity to teach him the pain of rejection?

Have you ever felt the sting of rejection? If so, in what way has that rejection affected your life?

____

____

Read Ephesians 3:2–6 again.

In verse 3, Paul states there was something made known to him. What was it?

Was this "mystery" revealed to men in other generations?

Ephesians 3:6 reveals the "mystery" Paul has uncovered. What is that mystery?

In Ephesians 3:2–6, Paul is stating that he has been given the understanding of one of God's mysteries. He's been entrusted with a secret that the Old Testament prophecies only alluded to. And now, God has made his plan known to Paul. His divine plan is that the Gentiles will now be united with Israel (the Jews) and will share in a relationship with the Lord.

You see, God spent the majority of the Old Testament period setting Israel apart from the other nations in order that the Messiah might come from Israel. But when Christ came, God's plan was to unite the Jews and Gentiles and then to join them both to God through Jesus Christ.

It's a wonderful plan, but consider the repercussions this plan had on the Gentiles, who for thousands of years had been rejected by God's people. How must they have felt during those years of estrangement? Always on the outside looking in, wondering what it must feel like to be listed among God's chosen few.

Do you suppose they suffered from rejection?

And if so, why do you suppose God allowed them to experience rejection?

Read John 4:7–9. Why was the Samaritan woman surprised that Jesus asked her for a drink?

The Samaritans were shunned by the Jews because they were originally Jews who had intermarried with Gentiles, thus creating Gentile descendants. It was because of this that the first-century Jews considered the Samaritans unclean.

Read John 4:28. After her discourse with Jesus, what did the Samaritan woman do?

Read John 4:39–42. How did these Gentiles respond to Christ in these verses?

Rejection teaches us conditional love. In the movie, *Hitch*, Alex Hitchens learns conditional love from Cressida. I learned conditional love from my first boyfriend and later in life, that lesson was validated by my college boyfriend. If we live long enough, we'll experience rejection because we're surrounded by humans. And human love is conditional. Human love grants or withholds affection based upon physical appearance, financial status, race, religion, or any other reason that comes to mind. But God's love is always unconditional.

The Samaritans were well versed in conditional love, because they'd suffered from rejection for hundreds of years. But their rejection had created within them a hunger for unconditional love. So they were receptive to the Savior when he came to Samaria.

You see, in those days, Samaria was located in the middle of Israel. Jews living in the northern region of Israel (Galilee) would journey south to Jerusalem to worship at the temple. But the Jews absolutely refused to pass through Samaria. In fact, they would journey many miles out of the way just to avoid Samaria and any interaction with the Samaritans. So when Christ traveled through

Samaria and actually spoke to the Samaritans, ministering to them and to their needs, the Samaritans immediately recognized his love, his *unconditional* love. This was the unconditional love and acceptance they'd been longing for for generations.

Earlier, I asked why you thought God allowed the Gentiles to experience rejection. And while I can't be certain of his reasons, all I know is that the Samaritans' rejection taught them conditional love. And their understanding of conditional love made them yearn for true love. It made them long for unconditional love–God's love.

When we experience rejection, we can do one of two things. We can build up walls of emotional apathy that keep our hearts locked and guarded so that we'll not be vulnerable to rejection again. Or we can be like the Samaritans and allow our rejection to create in us a longing for unconditional love–the kind of love that only Christ can provide.

My friend, what have you done with your rejection? Have you allowed it to imprison your heart, or have you allowed it to fuel your longing for unconditional love?

____

____

____

____

____

____

____

____

For many years my heart remained locked and guarded. But as I grew in Christ and traded the conditional love of humans for God's unconditional love, the ice around my heart slowly began to thaw. I now understand that rejection has purpose. It teaches us to hunger for unconditional love, and it also teaches us the amazing power of God's love. For it is his love that reaches past our emotional walls and breathes new life into our dormant hearts.

Prayer–*Lord, rejection is painful. It hurts and though I'd like to avoid it at all costs, I'm certain I'll experience it again before my life on earth is complete. So when that happens and conditional love rears its ugly head, give me the strength to take that rejection and give it to you. Give me the faith to believe that though others reject me, "the Lord will receive me" (Psalm 27:10). And let me trust in your unconditional love for me.*

Day 3: God's Love Revealed without Guile

Read Ephesians 3:7–13.

"With no guile and no game, there's no girl."
– Hitch[1]

The bar is crowded, but Hitch spots her. She is enjoying her position as the lone female in a crowd of attentive men. She is most definitely beautiful. And the mob of males surrounding her gives evidence of the fact that Hitch is not her sole admirer. Their presence makes his approach a little difficult, but he has a plan. He is a master at this, able to run game in any situation.

Approaching her with a confident air, Hitch feigns indifference as he pulls a twenty dollar bill from his pocket. He shoulders his way past her besotted posse and slips the money in her hand. Her eyes focus on the money, but

1. Kevin Bisch, "Albert." *Hitch*. DVD. Directed by Andy Tennant. Culver City, CA: Columbia Pictures, 2005.

when she looks up, his back is all she sees. His request for two Coronas with lime wedges propels her to action.

In frustration, she leaves her admirers in pursuit of Hitch. With money in hand, she waves him down to explain she doesn't work there. It is then that he knows he has her. So with guile in his eyes and a smile on his face, Hitch lets her know he is aware of her position, or lack thereof. He was just trying to get her alone, and now he's accomplished his task.

Basic Principle:

A guy has to have game when he's going after the girl. He's gotta give her enough to let her know he's interested, but he can't give her too much. Too much too soon isn't game, it's just being gullible. But a little guile and a little game will eventually get you the girl.

According to Ephesians 3:7, how did Paul become a servant of the gospel?

____

____

In Ephesians 3:8–9, Paul cites two reasons why God has granted him grace. What two reasons does he give?

____

____

Refer back to Ephesians 3:6, what is the mystery Paul is called to make plain?

____

____

In Day 1, we learned how God's love is revealed through Paul's suffering. In Day 2, we discovered how God's love is revealed in spite of rejection. And now, in Day 3, I just want us to embrace the fact that God's love is so plainly revealed.

Consider the Gentiles in Ephesus. God wasn't running game with them, he wasn't being coy or playing hard to get. God was forthright in his pursuit of them. God had opened up his heart to them. He'd given them Paul as a messenger of his love and kindness. He'd offered them a place in his kingdom alongside his chosen people. He'd given them his Son and he'd provided them the opportunity to reflect his wisdom and glory.

According to Ephesians 3:10–11, what was God's intent?

Understand that God's plan for humanity is unfolding upon two stages. The first and most apparent is the physical, earthly stage where we sit as the audience. And the second is the spiritual stage, where God's actions are viewed by a host of angelic and demonic spectators. Both audiences were created by God, and both have been given the option to receive or reject his love (see Jude 1:6a and 2 Peter 2:4).

According to Revelation 12:4, one-third of the angels rejected God's love and followed Satan in his rebellion against the creator. Since 2 Peter 2:4 says, "God did not spare angels when they sinned, but sent them to hell," we can conclude that redemption through Jesus Christ is not available to these fallen angels as it is to mankind.

Read John 8:44. How does Jesus describe Satan in this passage?

Since the Garden of Eden, Satan's been deceiving us with his lies, intent upon enticing us away from the Lord's love. His deception promises us power and pleasure, but beneath his guile is destruction.

With this in mind, reread Ephesians 3:10–11. Why do you suppose it was so important for God to make his revelation known to the rulers and authorities in the heavenly realms?

I think it's important because God's not using guile in his pursuit of us. He's had a plan since the beginning of time. Though that plan has unfolded progressively, he's not being deceitful in his dealings with us. He is aggressively and unashamedly pursuing humanity with his love. And by including the Gentiles in his overall plan, he has allowed anyone, from any race and any walk of life, the opportunity to enter into a love relationship with him.

This is what God wanted the rulers and authorities in the heavenly realms to recognize. He wanted them to see his boundless love for every individual. And he wanted them to see that love communicated without guile, deceit, or game. Perhaps he wanted them to know that despite their evil efforts, game and guile don't get the Gentile. Game and guile don't get God's people, because his love draws us in a way that no devious deception ever could.

Movie Trivia Question

- Consider Albert and Allegra's relationship. In the end, did game and guile get Allegra Cole?

Precious friend, even now, you are being wooed by two competing powers. One goes after you with game and guile, but he only offers destruction. The other goes after you with unfettered abandon. And with heart in hand, he offers you a love like no other. So whose advances will you respond to? Whose affections will you receive? And how will your decision shape your life?

Prayer—*Father God, I must admit that I'm faintly attracted to a little game and guile. Sometimes your love seems so easy, and when love is given so freely, it's often taken for granted. Forgive me God for taking your love for granted. Let me not be drawn to the deceitful advances of the enemy, and let me never choose power and pleasure over intimacy with you.*

Day 4: God's Love Revealed So We Might Receive It

Read Ephesians 3:14–19

Basic Principle:

No one knows how great love happens. It just does. "One moment, you're enjoying your life. And the next, you're wondering how you ever lived without them."

- Hitch[2]

Exactly how does great love happen? Hitch may have been unaware of the process, but the apostle Paul certainly knew the formula. And he reveals it to us in his prayer for the Ephesians. So let's study today's verses to see the process by which great love is produced!

Read Ephesians 3:14–17 and answer the following questions:

Who is Paul praying to?

____

____

____

What does Paul ask God to do in verse 16?

____

____

____

____

2. Bisch, "Start." *Hitch.* DVD.

According to that same verse, what member of the trinity will God use to strengthen us with power?

The first portion of verse 17 gives us the reason for Paul's request. What is the reason?

Paul manages to pack all three members of the Trinity into his rather potent prayer. In verses 16 and 17, he asks God to grant *permission* for the saints to receive power. Next, Paul acknowledges that the Holy Spirit will be the *process* by which that power is administered. Then finally in verse 17, Paul reveals the purpose for his request. The whole reason he asks the Father for power is so the *presence* of Christ might dwell in the hearts of God's people.

God the Father grants the *permission,* while the Holy Spirit enables the *process* by which the *presence* of Christ might dwell in our hearts. Sounds like a lot of "p" words, but that's only the beginning. Because the most significant word in Paul's prayer is the word "power."

Read Ephesians 3:16–19 and notice Paul's two requests for power.

According to verses 16–17, why was power needed?

According to verses 18–19, why was power needed?

____

____

____

I must admit, I read these verses and wonder, "Why such a need for power?" Why can't Christ just dwell in my heart? I've already asked him to, so why can't he just do it? And why do I need power to know the full extent of Christ's love for me? Power. It seems an odd escort for love.

Hitch is a master at creating opportunities for others to fall in love. His advice helps guys understand that even beautiful women often fail to know their hearts' desire until it is standing right before their eyes. So Hitch feels it his noble duty to help women see. And throughout his career, he's done a rather remarkable job of it.

Yet though his expertise with women has given him quite a high volume of clientele, his experiences with the opposite sex have come at a cost. And he is still paying restitution. For beneath his confident façade lays a heart held captive by past hurts and failed relationships. And he doesn't have the power to break free.

The word "power" in verses 16 and 18 is translated from the Greek word *dunamis* meaning, "ability or strength."[3] It's a word used quite frequently by the writers of the New Testament, and it's often associated with the Holy Spirit. The two are often used in tandem, because the Holy Spirit enables the process by which power is administered to God's people.

3. Thayer and Smith. "Greek Lexicon entry for Dunamis," *The New Testament Greek Lexicon.* (The Lockman Foundation, 1998). <http://www.studylight.org/lex/grk/view.cgi?number=1411>.

After having read Paul's prayer for the Ephesians in chapter 3, why do you suppose the Christians in Ephesus would have needed power to assist them in their love relationship with Christ?

____

____

____

____

In Day 2 we examined the pain associated with conditional love and rejection. Then in Day 3, we considered the enemy's tendency to *deceive* God's people, attracting us with his guile. So with conditional love, rejection and guile factored into our understanding of love, it's no wonder we, as Christians, need God's supernatural power and ability to receive Christ's love.

If you'll notice, everything about Paul's prayer places us as recipients. Paul's not praying we produce love or orchestrate a relationship with Christ. He's not asking God to make us better Christians so we might love Christ more fully. He's merely asking that we receive–that we receive Christ's love for us.

In verse 16, Paul asks that we be given power so we might receive Christ into our hearts, allowing our Savior to take up residence there. Then in verses 18–19, he requests that we receive knowledge and understanding of Christ's great love for us.

I have three daughters, and every night as I tuck them into bed, I pray over them. I used to pray, "Lord, give them a heart that loves you." And while I still pray that prayer, I've found the need to add an additional clause to that request. So now, as my eight-year-old lays in her daybed and my four- and six-year-olds snuggle together in their double bed, I touch each of them praying that God would give them hearts that love him, and hearts that receive his love in return.

I pray this because I've discovered that in my own life, much of my spiritual struggles did not result from a lack of love for Christ. Many of my difficulties stemmed from my inability to receive his love for me.

Sometimes I failed to receive my Savior's love because of my own pride. Because I wanted to earn it instead of accept it. Other times, my experiences with rejection and conditional love convinced me that Christ's love would cease if I did something wrong. I guess I assumed his love came with conditions, so I was hesitant to fully receive it. You see, a love with conditions is quite often a short-term affair.

I'm still growing in Christ, but I've sinned often enough to understand that his love remains–despite my failures. I'm forever tempted to work for his love, endeavoring to earn it through good works or deeds. But though my temptations exist and my failures persist, I am convinced of this: God loves me, and I need his power daily just to muster the faith to receive his love.

How about you? How do you daily receive Christ's awesome, immeasurable love for you?

A few years ago, I spoke on this very topic. And at the conclusion of my message, I sang the lyrics to a song I wrote. (By the way, I'm a horrible singer, and the fact that I sang the song *a cappella* made the whole experience less than enjoyable for my audience. I have, unfortunately, never been asked to speak at that church again. So now I limit my solos to the shower!) Anyway, here's the song, I pray it's received better in print than it was in person.

I Am Loved By You

> I am loved by you. No one else can love me quite like you do. Despite the trials and the heartaches of life, you prove, I am loved by you.
>
> Your love is a well that will never run dry. It reaches the depths of my soul. So give me the power to open my heart and receive your gift to me.
>
> For I am loved by you. No one else can love me quite like you do. Despite the trials and the heartaches of life, you prove, I am loved by you.

So how does great love happen? Well, according to Paul, it takes all three members of the Godhead and a supernatural power to pull it off. But in the end, it happens, and we are the richer for it. Great love: first a great God gives it, and then we as gracious saints supernaturally receive it.

Prayer–*Oh God, please give me the power to receive your love. For only your power will free my heart from my fear of rejection. And only your supernatural strength will release me from the temptation to earn your love. So grant me your power, I pray, for once I am free, then can I truly receive your unconditional love for me.*

Day 5: God's Love Revealed so He Might Receive Glory

Read Ephesians 3:20–21.

The steps to Sara's apartment have never seemed so steep, but here he is: climbing after her and planning to make a fool of himself once he reaches the apex. Momentarily, he gives her door a cheerful knock while he smiles and waves at the peephole. He knows she sees him because she thrusts the door open and leans against it to bar his entrance. Her lips are drawn in a tight, thin line, and the glare she gives him conveys her displeasure.

Smiling, Hitch tries to warm her frigid greeting with nervous laughter, but she refuses to thaw. Between her icy presence and his fear of rejection, Hitch finds himself completely befuddled. Words that had once so effortlessly flowed from his lips with wit and charm, are now jumbled and disoriented. He doesn't know what to say or how to say it. It has been years since he's made himself this vulnerable in love and now he's forgotten the art of groveling.

Though Sara's aura radiates impatience and annoyance, still he tries, fumbling for the right words to say. But his attempts to win her back come to an abrupt halt when she opens the door further, revealing the presence of a tall, attractive, male stranger. She introduces the brute, but Hitch doesn't catch the name. He is too busy considering the repercussions this guy's presence has on his chances at love.

The stranger makes his way out of the apartment with Sara's bags in hand. Following in his wake, Sara steps through the portal, locking the door behind her. Turning, she faces Hitch and reminds him of his past suggestion that they both go their separate ways, for surely if they do, everything will work out just fine.

Her final words spoken, she turns and begins her descent to the corridor. And as she does so, the steady rhythm of Hitch's heart echoes her footfall.

He has to stop her. So standing at the top of the landing he calls to her, "What if fine isn't good enough? What if I want extraordinary?"[4]

Basic Principle:

Fine isn't good enough. When it comes to love, only the extraordinary, only the immeasurable, only the unimaginable will do.

Read Ephesians 3:20.

What is God able to do?

___

___

___

___

How is he able to do it?

___

___

___

In Day 4, we learned that we need God's power in order to fully receive Christ's love for us. Once we've received God's power and Christ's love, then we're faced with a new challenge. The challenge is beginning a new life with a perfect God dwelling in our often fickle hearts while we walk the streets of a sinful world. With this challenge before us, a love relationship with Christ seems a difficult one to sustain. It would be doomed from the outset, if not for God's power working within us.

4. Bisch, "The Leap." *Hitch*. DVD.

Thankfully, the same power that gives us the ability to receive Christ's love also gives us the ability to sustain a relationship with Almighty God. God has granted us that power through the Holy Spirit. And when that power is exercised in our lives, he's able to join with it and make our relationship with Christ extraordinary, immeasurable, and unimaginable.

But what is an unimaginable relationship with Christ? What does it entail? And what does it look like? Let's end our week together discovering what happens when we refuse to settle for a mere "fine" relationship with the divine. So join me in my pursuit of an extraordinary relationship with Christ and allow God's power within us to produce the unimaginable.

Write the first sentence of 1 John 4:16.

____

____

____

____

Before we can truly allow God's power to do extraordinary things through us, we must first apply the lesson we learned in Day 4. We must receive God's unconditional love. We must know it, believe it, and rely on it.

I was browsing through scripture the other day during my quiet time and I found this wonderful verse. It's about God's unfailing love. The New International Version reads, "The Lord delights in those who fear him, who put their hope in his unfailing love" (Psalm 147:11).

I want the Lord to delight in me. I want him to know that I fear him. But more than that, I want him to know that I believe he loves me. I receive that love, and I'm putting all my hope and all my trust in it.

Why do you suppose it's so important that we, as the bride of Christ, put our faith in his unfailing love?

Read David's words in Psalm 13.

How did David feel about God at the outset of this psalm?

He had a change of heart in verse 5. According to this verse, in what does David trust?

The Hebrew word translated "trust" in this verse is *batach,* and it means "to be secure" or "to feel safe."[5] David was so safe and secure in God's love for him, that even amid all his trials and frustrations with God, he still knew God loved him. He still trusted in God's

5. Brown, Driver, Briggs, and Gesenius. "Hebrew Lexicon entry for Batach," *The Old Testament Hebrew Lexicon* (The Lockman Foundation, 1998). <http://www.studylight.org/lex/heb/view.cgi?number=982>.

unfailing love for him. That, my friend is an extraordinary, unimaginable relationship!

When we fully grasp the depth of our Savior's love for us, when we accept that love and feel safe and secure within it, then our trials here on earth seem only temporary and completely irrelevant in light of our eternal relationship with God. Sure, sometimes God's distant behavior is maddening, at least for me it is. And I'm sure that if I were to interview our Lord, he'd say similar things about my behavior. But that is the essence of relationship. Sometimes it's fraught with misunderstandings and miscommunications. Sometimes it's filled with delight and other times, disappointment. (I know I've certainly experienced disappointments in my relationship with the Lord.)

But through it all, one thing remains–his unfailing love. And it's in that love we must place our trust, find our security, and discover our safety. For when we do, God does an amazing thing.

Read Ephesians 3:21. Paul ends his prayer with this verse. But what does he pray God will receive through the church and through Christ Jesus?

____

____

____

____

When we embark upon a relationship with Christ, he extends his love to us. God's Holy Spirit within us gives us the power to receive that love. Then God takes our relationship with his son and does immeasurably more than all we ask or imagine. Through it all, God receives the glory.

Because God garners praise and glory from our relationship with Christ, it's important that we don't settle for mediocrity. For us, fine isn't good enough. When it comes to our love relationship with

Christ, only the extraordinary, only the immeasurable, only the unimaginable will do. So believe and receive and in the process, allow God his glory.

Prayer–*God, thanks for giving me permission to receive Christ's love for me. I receive all kinds of things from the enemy: guilt, condemnation, remorse. So often I feel unworthy of such love lavished upon me by your precious son. But today, I choose to receive that love, to feel secure in it and to put my trust in it. And Lord, as I grow in my relationship with Christ, may our love reflect your glory.*

HIS RESPONSIVE BRIDE

Ephesians 4

VOW: "From him the whole body, joined and held together by every supporting ligament, grows and builds itself up in love, as each part does its work."	**Ephesians 4:16**

Day 1: Responding with Unity

Read Ephesians 4:1–6.

The final scene of *Hitch* reveals the stars of the movie entertaining the crowd of wedding goers with their hilarious moves on the dance floor. According to Eva Mendes, who played the role of Sara Melas, the dance moves were "all improvised. None of that was choreographed for anybody. We were just like, 'Okay, let's just act like idiots on the dance floor. Who can out-idiot each other!'"[1]

Their idiotic gyrations were comical, as they kept beat to Heavy D's remake of the O'Jay's song, "Now That We Found Love." During

1. Stella Papamichael, "Movies, Interviews: Eva Mendes," *BBC*, March 1, 2005, http://www.bbc.co.uk/films/2005/03/01/eva_mendes_hitch_interview.shtml.

the disco era, the O'Jay's burst on the scene with this upbeat song that continually questions what we should do with love, now that we've discovered it.

It's a great question to ask ourselves–what will we do with love, especially since we've spent the last several weeks studying God's infinite love for us. His love has offered us eternal life, holiness, and righteousness. His love has chosen us, called us, pursued us, and united us with his people. In addition to all this, his love has given us his son, thus making us the bride of Christ. So what shall we do, now that we've found love?

Read Ephesians 4:1. What does Paul encourage us to do in this verse?

____

____

____

Paul spent the first three chapters of Ephesians revealing the infinite love of God and the great gifts God has bestowed on us. Now, in Ephesians 4:1, Paul encourages us to respond to the love we've received. And he spends the final three chapters of Ephesians explaining what our response to God should look like.

Movie Mania

To better understand this study of Ephesians 4, watch *13 Going on 30* and consider the following questions:

- At the outset of the movie, how did Jenna respond to Matt's affection?
- What did it take for Jenna to respond to Matt's love?

According to Ephesians 4:2–3, what are some ways we can respond to God's love?

Observe these attributes closely, for all of them are necessary in our relationships with others. Of course, they are beneficial in our relationship with God, but they are absolutely essential in our associations with others in the faith.

Paul goes on in verses 4–6 to explain why it is so important that we respond to God's love with humility and patience.

What word is repeated over and over again in these verses?

According to this repeated word, why is it so important that Christians be humble and maintain the unity of the Spirit?

Review Ephesians 2:19–22, why is it so important for Christians to be unified?

____

____

____

Jenna has always wanted a Barbie Dream House, so Matt gives her one on her thirteenth birthday. It's not exactly a Barbie house, but rather a modified version of one. He calls it a Jenna Dream House and it's taken him three weeks to build. He's included everything she loves within the four walls of the house–her music, her magazines, and even her bubble bath. And for good measure, he's included a picture of himself.

After presenting his gift to her, he sprinkles wishing dust on the dream house in hopes that all of Jenna's dreams will come true. And that one day, she'll get her real dream house.

As Christians, you and I are God's dream house. We constitute his ultimate abode. In the Old Testament, he limited his presence on earth to a physical structure, the Temple. But now, he lives in us, individually and corporately. He takes up residence within the hearts of his saints.

Though the Jews of the Old Testament were never granted God's presence the way we are, 2 Chronicles records a foreshadowing of God's ultimate dream home. In 2 Chronicles, King Solomon enlists the assistance of the King of Tyre for the building of the temple. Tyre was a pagan land where only Gentiles lived, and its borders flanked God's chosen nation, Israel. During the reigns of King David and King Solomon, the countries were allies. And in 2 Chronicles 2, Solomon writes a letter to King Hiram, the ruler of Tyre. In his letter, the wise Solomon petitions King Hiram for a master craftsman to work in Jerusalem with Israel's skilled craftsmen. Yet Solomon had further plans for his Jewish nation and this Gentile kingdom.

Read 2 Chronicles 2:8, what did Solomon say regarding the men of Israel and the men of Tyre?

____

____

Little did they know that hundreds of years later, both Jews and Gentiles would reunite for the construction of yet another temple. This time it would be a home, a dream home, comprised of Christ's followers in which God lives by his Spirit. But in order for this building project to work, it was essential that every person–Jew and Gentile alike–play their part and that everyone be unified.

To unify the church, Paul first instructs us in Ephesians 4:2 to be humble. I love how Warren Wiersbe describes humility in his book, *Be Rich.* He writes,

> Humility means putting Christ first, others second, and self last. It means knowing ourselves, accepting ourselves, and being ourselves to the glory of God. God does not condemn you when you accept yourself and your gifts (Romans 12:3). He just does not want us to think more highly of ourselves than we ought to–or less highly than we ought to.[2]

The next quality Paul encourages us to pursue is gentleness or meekness. In today's society, meekness is often misunderstood for weakness. However, nothing could be further from the truth. Meekness is "power under control."[3] The Greek word for meekness is *prautetos,* a word the Greeks used to describe a horse that had been broken. Meekness is demonstrated in the life of Christ. He was an incredibly powerful man, fully aware of his authority and ability, yet he did not allow his power to control him. Instead, he controlled it.

2. Warren W. Wiersbe, *Be Rich* (Colorado Springs, CO: Cook Communications, 2004), 95.
3. Ibid.

In Ephesians 4, Paul's intent is to unite the body of Christ. Why would humility and meekness be necessary characteristics for this unification process?

The third directive Paul gives is that we be patient, bearing with one another in love. In the Greek New Testament, there are two words translated as the English word "patience." The first is *hupomone* and refers to patience in respect to trials or things. The second is *makrothumia* and refers to patience in respect to people. The Greek word Paul used in this passage is *makrothumia.* "Bearing with one another in love" is a form of *makrothumia.* Commentator Kenneth S. Wuest describes a man of patience as, "he who, having to do with injurious persons, does not suffer himself easily to be provoked by them or to blaze up in anger."[4]

Paul's fourth desire is for the church to *keep the unity of the Spirit* through the bond of peace. The Holy Spirit dwelling within our spirits is what unites us. Yet we are three-part beings: body, soul, and spirit. Our spirits may be in agreement with one another due to the infilling of the Holy Spirit, but our souls will often be in conflict. Our souls are the part of us that comprise our minds, wills, and emotions. As we mature in Christ, our minds, wills, and emotions will conform to the Holy Spirit within us. But until that time, others in the body of Christ may have to exert a great deal of *makrothumia* in order to put up with us.

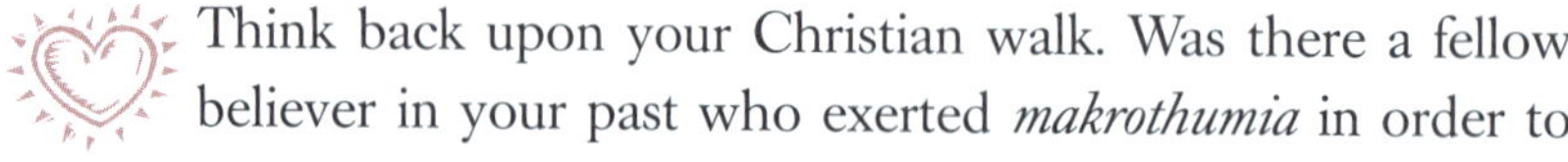

Think back upon your Christian walk. Was there a fellow believer in your past who exerted *makrothumia* in order to

4. Kenneth S. Wuest, *Wuest's Word Studies from the Greek New Testament: Volume I* (Grand Rapids, MI: Wm. B. Eerdmans Publishing Company, 1973), 95.

mature you in Christ? If so, who were they, and what impact has their influence had on your life?

____

____

____

____

____

My spiritual growth required massive amounts of *makrothumia* on my parents' behalf. I was a rather strong-willed child to say the least. But don't worry, God is a just God, and he's made sure that my children behave in such a way so as to exercise my *makrothumia*!

Along with my parents, my youth pastor played an influential role in my spiritual development. Our souls sparred on numerous occasions–because for some reason, he didn't like to be told what to do. Nonetheless, despite my immaturity, he never allowed the unity of the Spirit to be broken. I still remained his sister in Christ, a childish, adolescent sister, but a sister.

Because the body of Christ has embarked upon a spiritual building project, the apostle Paul wrote his epistle to ensure we weren't divided by the conflicts of our souls. Strife and division hinder our efforts to create an earthly dwelling place for the Most High God. So Paul encourages us to remember the one thing that unites us–the Spirit.

Prayer–*Lord, thank you for the opportunity to be a part of your holy temple. Thank you that I get to labor alongside my brothers and sisters in the faith for the formation of your dwelling place. Let our home be a harmonious place for you to live. Let us not be divided by petty strife and rivalry, but instead, let our humility, patience, unity, and love be the foundation of your dream home.*

Day 2: Responding with Service

Read Ephesians 4:7–12.

Reread verse 7.

What was given to us?

And who gave it?

In Ephesians 4:8–10, Paul states why Christ has the authority to give his gift of grace to believers. The apostle quotes the Old Testament and cites Christ's authority to bestow gifts by explaining Christ's ascension. But today, instead of focusing on Christ's authority, let's focus on his gifts of grace and his reasons for giving them.

According to Ephesians 4:11, what gifts of grace does Christ give believers?

Further listings of the gifts of the Spirit can be found in Romans 12:6–8 and 1 Corinthians 12:8–10. Review these passages and list some additional spiritual gifts.

There are numerous gifts of the Spirit identified by Paul in the New Testament and each one serves a specific purpose. According to 1 Corinthians 12:7, gifts of the Spirit are given for the common good. Paul continues in the twelfth chapter of Corinthians to draw a metaphor of the body, comparing it to the church and identifying its varying parts. Each body part is essential, just as each member of the body of Christ is essential. Each member is gifted by the Spirit and is called to contribute an important service to the rest of the body.

According to Ephesians 4:12a the gifts of apostleship, prophecy, evangelism, and teaching develop the body of Christ by preparing God's people for what?

Because we are a part of the body of Christ, each of us is called to serve the body in some form or fashion. God provides us pastors and teachers and evangelists to prepare us for these works of service. God also gives us varying spiritual gifts to assist us in our service to the body.

Matt's presentation of Jenna's Dream House is interrupted by the sound of the doorbell. Jenna knows it's the Six Chicks and she's filled with nervous excitement. She glances around the room to ensure everything is perfect. But before she flies upstairs to welcome her guests of honor, she spies Matt's gift. The dream house is too bulky. It has to go. So she shoves it in a closet, concealing it from view.

What is Jenna's gift, and what does she do with it?

What are your spiritual gifts and what are you doing with them?

Since God has lavished his love on us, one of the ways we can respond to his love is through works of service. When we recognize and exercise our spiritual gifts, God enables us to use these gifts to serve the body of Christ, causing the body to be built up and edified (Ephesians 4:12).

Two and a half years ago, my husband and I joined with a pastor and his wife in planting a church. It has proven to be a huge undertaking, but we've grown so much through the whole process. During these formative years of our church, we've maintained a vision of what our church might look like. And our vision mirrors Paul's description of the body of Christ in 1 Corinthians 12. It is a vision where each member uses his/her gift to serve the body.

At our church, no one is exempt from service. We don't own a building, so each week we set up and break down. And most everyone, from the oldest to the youngest, assists in this process. From the strongest men carrying the baptismal pool to the two- and three-year-olds pulling containers of toys down the hall, everyone plays a part.

In addition to the physical labor everyone offers, there's also an expectation for everyone to contribute spiritually as well. So as leaders of the church, we try to help people identify their spiritual gifts. And then we attempt to foster these gifts in them. For instance, if someone has the gift of wisdom, we try to make them aware of that gift and encourage them to grow in that gift and to use it to edify others in the body.

If someone has the gift of teaching, then we provide teachers' training seminars so they can learn how to study the Bible. This enables them to accurately handle the Word of God whenever they teach. Furthermore, we encourage them to use their gift by providing opportunities for them to teach in small groups and Bible studies.

For the most part, our church members have been very receptive to this method of "doing church." And they've invited their friends, bolstering our church growth to about three hundred people in less than three years. Yet despite our growth, we've noticed that people with a consumer-driven view of Christianity don't like our church very much. People who maintain the mentality of extracting without the intent of contributing do not stick around for very long. And perhaps that is for the best, since the church was meant to function as a body, with each member contributing, serving, and using their gifts to bless other members of the body.

Prayer–*Lord, I feel so fulfilled when I use my spiritual gifts in service to you and others within the body of Christ. It is often scary and intimidating to step out in faith and exercise the gifts you've given me. But when I do, the end result is so rewarding. Please grant me the courage to continue using these gifts and the grace to receive the gifts of others in return.*

Day 3: Responding with Growth

Read Ephesians 4:13–16.

In Ephesians 4:12, Paul says that pastors and Bible teachers are given in order to prepare God's people for works of service so the body of Christ may mature. Then in Ephesians 4:13, Paul describes what maturity in the body of Christ looks like. According to this verse, what is the goal?

Read Ephesians 4:14. What will happen as a result of our spiritual growth?

The goal is that we all mature so that we are confident in our faith and are no longer deceived by false doctrine. According to the apostle Paul, maturity occurs when we reach unity in the faith and in the knowledge of Christ and attain to the whole measure of the fullness of Christ. We attain unity in the faith and in the knowledge of Christ when we exercise our faith, trusting Christ to lead us and guide us and perform amazing things through us. As we exercise our faith in him, we become more knowledgeable of him and of his ways. We increase in our understanding of the Son of God. However, what does Paul mean when he writes we must attain to the whole measure of the fullness of Christ?

Read Ephesians 4:15–16. According to verse 15, who are we to grow up in to?

____

____

It seems a rather hopeless endeavor to grow up into the divine Messiah. But that is what Paul instructs believers to do. In verse 13 he tells us to attain to the whole measure of the fullness of Christ, which in my opinion is just another way of saying, "grow up into Christ." Long to be like him. Hold him as your life's goal. Strive to be an exact replica of him.

Jenna hates her life. Being an awkward 13-year-old is boring and uneventful. The women she sees in Poise *magazine were exciting and glamorous. They had moved beyond braces, middle school, and parental control. They were strong, independent thirty-year-olds. They were "flirty and thriving." They had reached the apex of life, and Jenna longs to join them. So on her thirteenth birthday she makes a wish. And much to Jenna's surprise, it comes true.*

Movie Trivia Question

- What is Jenna's wish?

It doesn't seem possible. She is thirteen years old. Or at least she had been while in the closet. But when she opens her eyes again, she finds herself in an unfamiliar apartment–with an unfamiliar, drop-dead gorgeous body. The mirror she peers at reveals an attractive, but foreign face. What has happened to her hair, her makeup, her figure? It has all changed. Who is she? Where is she? And what has become of her wiry, thirteen-year-old frame?

I wish I could be like Jenna, magically wishing my immaturity away and suddenly becoming the object of my desire. I wish I could forgo the maturation process and mystically become like Christ. But I can't. So here I sit, on the road of spiritual growth with Christ as my ultimate destination. I could go back, but Paul says in Philippians 4:16 that we are to "live up to what we have already attained." So there goes that option.

I could remain where I'm at, content with my spiritual growth thus far. But in reality, there's no such thing as nongrowth. We'll grow one way or another. Either we'll grow closer to our goal, which is Christ, or we'll grow further from him. But either way, we'll grow. So we might as well be like Paul and "press on toward the goal" (Philippians 3:14). We might as well accept the challenge and grow toward Christ.

My friend, I hope and pray you'll accept the challenge and respond to God's love with growth. And if you do, there is something I want you to know. God isn't asking anything of us that he hasn't already asked of Christ.

How is Christ described in the following verses?

• Luke 2:40

• Luke 2:52

Read Mark 14:32–36. What was Christ's prayer in verses 35–36?

____

____

____

Being fully God and fully man, Christ endured the maturation process just like us. Not only did he encounter physical growth, but he had to respond to God with spiritual and emotional growth as well.

According to James 1:2–4, what does God use to grow and mature us?

____

____

____

According to Hebrews 2:10, how did God make Christ perfect?

____

____

____

The Greek word translated "perfect" in this passage is perhaps better translated as, "to make complete."[5] The word "perfect" isn't suggesting Christ was at one time sinful and needed to be made pure. It suggests that God had a work for Christ to do, and in order to complete that work, God allowed his son to undergo suffering. But the suffering had purpose. It brought about growth, growth in Christ and growth within the body of Christ.

5. James Strong, *Strong's Exhaustive Concordance of the Bible* (Nashville, TN: Royal Publishers, 1947) 71.

How do you view spiritual growth? Do you view it as a necessary evil, or do you embrace it as an opportunity to become more like Christ?

When I look at growth, or rather, my need for spiritual growth, I see deficiencies. I see shortcomings that need to be remedied. But that's not God's view of growth. God views our growth, not in light of our deficiencies, but rather in light of our possibilities. He sees the finished project. He sees us becoming more and more like Christ.

I wish we could be like Jenna and just skip all the trials and suffering. But that is an essential part of the maturation process. It is the suffering that produces perseverance in our lives, and this perseverance leads to spiritual maturity.

Prayer–*Lord, give me the grace to grow spiritually. Let me not become complacent in my spiritual journey. But help me be encouraged by the fact that Christ walked this road to maturity just like me. It is he who paved the way, so now all I need do is follow.*

Day 4: Responding with a Pliable Heart

Read Ephesians 4:17–19

As a thirty-year-old, Jenna doesn't remember anything beyond the night of her 13th birthday party, but Matt does. At Jenna's insistence, Matt explains the events of their teen years and the demise of their relationship. He also informs Jenna of his engagement, introducing her to his fiancée, Wendy. Initially, Jenna receives this information with childlike wonder, but as the movie progresses, Jenna realizes that her feelings for Matt go beyond mere friendship.

In Day 3 we studied spiritual growth and God's desire that we mature in Christ. We discovered that God's ultimate goal is that we grow up and become like Christ. Today we will discover a major hindrance to our spiritual growth. Paul's verses for today are filled with caution. And he introduces his caveat with an analysis of the Gentiles.

Read Ephesians 4:17–19. Describe how the Gentiles lived.

____

____

____

The unsaved Gentiles of Ephesus engaged in a wide array of folly, but if we look closely at Paul's writings, we'll see *why* they fell prey to such ignorance. Why they were darkened in their understanding. Why they were separated from the life of God. And why they gave themselves over to "every kind of impurity."

Review Ephesians 4:17–19 and answer the question, "Why?"

____

____

In the midst of encouraging the Ephesians to live holy lives, Paul inserts a warning for them not to live with hardened hearts as the Gentiles did. He would not have inserted this warning had it not been possible for the Ephesians to fall prey to a hardened, callous heart.

Jenna races up the stairs of Matt's childhood home. Reaching the second floor, she pauses by the open door to consider the bride who stands within the portal. Wendy's gown is beautiful; she is beautiful, and Matt has claimed her as his own. But Jenna has to tell him the truth about her feelings for him. She has to let him know the truth she's discovered deep within her heart, the truth that has eluded her for so many years. She has to tell him that she loves him.

Read Jeremiah 17:9. Why is it possible for Christians to fall prey to hardened hearts?

____

____

____

After her emotional plea to Matt, Jenna leaves him to his final wedding preparations. He is kind enough to give her the dream house he made for her on her thirteenth birthday. But that is all he offers. His love and affection he reserves for Wendy.

Jenna escapes the wedding party, carrying her dream home with her. She settles close by, listening to the wedding music as she examines her dream home. The pink house with its blue shutters and its picture of Matt contains everything Jenna wants, but can never have. The familiar sound of the bridal march reaches Jenna's ears and she realizes, she's gotten every wish her thirteen-year-old heart desired, but in the end, her heart had deceived her.

Our hearts are prone to deception. And without Christ, our hearts are prone to sin. All sin is deceptive. The pagan Gentiles Paul refers to in this passage were ignorant of their own sin. In fact, they didn't even recognize they were sinning. Cautious that this plight might befall the Christian Ephesians, Paul warns them of the symptom of a hardened heart.

Read Ephesians 4:19a. What is the symptom of a hardened heart?

____

____

The King James Version renders this portion of scripture as: "being past feeling." John Wesley writes, "The original word is peculiarly significant. It properly means, " 'past feeling pain.' Pain urges the sick to seek a remedy, which, where there is no pain, is little thought of."[6]

At the outset of the movie, young Jenna operated under the deception of a hardened heart. She felt no pain for Matt, no remorse for the way she treated him. And as the story unfolds, it appears she lived with that hardened, deceptive heart for seventeen years.

King David displayed a hardened, callous heart when he committed adultery and murder in 2 Samuel 11. Apparently, he felt no pain from his sin, because he was not convicted of it. In fact, his hardened heart deceived him for *months*, causing him to believe he had done nothing wrong. It was not until God sent the prophet Nathan to confront David, that this man after God's own heart was capable of seeing his sin.

David wrote Psalm 51 in response to Nathan's rebuke. In it, he demonstrates a softened, pliable, repentant heart. Read this passage and describe what such a heart looks like.

____

____

6. John Wesley, "Commentary on Ephesians 4." In *John Wesley's Explanatory Notes on the Whole Bible,* 1765, http://www.studylight.org/com/wen/view.cgi?book =eph&chapter=004>.

Using Psalm 51, write your own prayer for a pure, pliable heart.

In Psalms 51:10, David petitions God to create in him a pure heart. David knew from experience the dangers a hardened, defiled heart could bring, so he asked God to give him a pure heart. He desired to respond to God with a pliable heart. But he knew he needed God's assistance. So he asked God for something else.

Read these passages and write down David's additional requests regarding his heart.

- Psalms 141:4

- Psalms 139:23–24

David knew a pliable heart would need two things: *protection* and *inspection.* Even though the natural tendency of our hearts is to be wayward and deceitful, David asked that his heart be protected from those things by being sheltered from the enticement of evil. David also understood that even if God granted his request in Psalms 51:10 and gave him a pure heart, that heart would still require constant inspection for sin.

As innate, sinful beings, we are incapable of adequately inspecting our hearts. Even the apostle Paul was incapable of judging himself. He wrote in 1 Corinthians 4:3–4: "I care very little if I am judged by you or by any human court; indeed, I do not even judge myself. My conscience is clear, but that does not make me innocent. It is the Lord who judges me."

In order to avoid a hardened heart, we need an experienced Inspector, one who can efficiently distinguish between good and bad, sin and righteousness. I've gotten myself into a great deal of turmoil by attempting to be my own inspector. I've lived under unnecessary guilt and shame when I misjudged an action as sinful when it really wasn't. Other times, I've been completely blinded to my own sin and been unable to identify it, let alone repent of it. And through all this I'm learning to let the Lord judge me, to trust him with my righteousness. But then he reminds me that my righteousness is as filthy rags and it is his responsibility to clothe me in purity and make me holy and blameless (see Isaiah 64:6; Ephesians 5:25–27; and Revelation 19:8).

Prayer–*Lord, thank you for being willing to protect my heart and to inspect my heart. Teach me to trust you with every part of me. And please Lord, help me always respond to you with a pliable heart.*

Day 5: Responding with the New Self

Read Ephesians 4:20–32.

Ephesians 4 is all about responding to God with unity and growth within the body of Christ. Unity in the body is established by way of the Spirit and the fruits of the Spirit produced in the lives of each member (Ephesians 4:1–3). Growth within the body is achieved through anointed apostles, prophets, evangelists, pastors, and teachers who mature God's people, preparing them for works of service (Ephesians 4:11–12). But unity and growth are also achieved through the wardrobe God gives Christ's body to wear.

Read Ephesians 4:20–22. According to verse 22, what "outfit" are we to take off? And how is that outfit described?

Read Ephesians 4:23–24. What "outfit" are we to put on? And how is that outfit described?

In the movie, *13 Going on 30,* Jennifer Garner's character, Jenna Rink, matures as the movie unfolds. To portray Jenna's emotional maturity, costume designer, Susie DeSanto, made sure the character's wardrobe was a reflection of the changes occurring within the heart of Jenna Rink.

In an interview with the designer, DeSanto states,

> Jennifer's character has a big character arch in how she changes and realizes who she is, and the costumes have to tell that story. Jenna as an adult works for a fabulous fashion magazine. These women who work in these places are obsessed with labels. . . . When she (Jenna) starts to kind of like realize her friendship with Matt and kind of get in touch with her sweetness and stuff like that, we started using a lot of pink and really pretty soft fabrics that Jenna as a 13 year old would actually pick out.[7]

As believers, we have a spiritual wardrobe. This outfit must reflect the changes occurring within our hearts. The pinks and soft fabrics of Jenna's new wardrobe are to me a reminder of the new "outfit" or garment the body of Christ is to wear. When we wear the garment of the old self, we are corrupted by deceitful desires and walk like the pagan Gentiles we studied in Day 4. But when we wear the garment of the new self, we reflect the image of God in true righteousness and holiness.

If you watch the movie again (or for the very first time), notice the change in Jenna's wardrobe as the movie progresses. But before you analyze Jenna's attire, let's first journey through Ephesians 4:25–32 to analyze our new spiritual wardrobe.

Read Ephesians 4:25–32. List the different aspects of our new wardrobe.

____

____

The first attribute that accents our new wardrobe is honesty–and not just honesty with ourselves, but honesty with other members of the body of Christ. According to David Guzik, "A body can only function properly if it tells itself the truth. If your hand touches some-

7. Christina Hacopian, "Making of a Teen Dream." *13 Going on 30: Special Addition.* DVD. Directed by Gary Winick. Culver City, CA: Columbia Pictures, 2004.

thing hot, but your hand tells your brain that the thing is cool, your hand will be severely burned. That's why telling the truth is so important, because we are members of one another."[8]

According to Ephesians 4:15, how are we to tell other Christians the truth?

According to 1 John 4:16, God is love, so in essence, we can only speak truth to our brothers and sisters in Christ when love permeates our words. Or another way to think of it is that we speak truth when God gives us permission to speak it. Truth always arouses emotion. Sometimes that emotion is good, other times it is bad. Even when spoken in love, truth can arouse anger within the heart of the hearer. Perhaps that is why Paul commissioned the Ephesians to be angry without sinning.

There will be times when other members of the body anger us. And while we have permission to *feel* that emotion, we do not have permission to *act* upon it. One way we can wear the new wardrobe God gives us is by putting a time limit on our anger. Paul writes in verse 26 that we are to limit our anger by not allowing the sun to go down while we are still angry. This time limit prevents the *feeling* of anger from becoming an *action.* It also prevents our anger from turning into bitterness.

Read Hebrews 12:15. What does a bitter root do?

8. David Guzik, "Commentary on Ephesians 4." In *David Guzik's Commentaries on the Bible* (2003). <http://www.studylight.org/com/guz/view.cgi?book=eph&chapter=004>.

I love what one commentator says about anger and bitterness. Guzik relates, "The devil's work is to accuse and divide the family of God, and to sow discord among them; when we harbor anger in our hearts, we are doing the devil's work for him."[9] By eradicating anger in its early stages, we prevent bitterness from defiling us and others around us, and best of all, we prevent the enemy from using us to divide the body of Christ.

Diligence and generosity are two more characteristics that adorn the new wardrobe we've received in Christ. In verse 28, Paul commissions the Ephesians to stop stealing and to work. But he did not want them to labor for their own needs; he wanted them to work in order to share and provide for the needs of others. Sharing one's possessions is a hallmark of the New Testament church.

Read Acts 2:44–45. What did the believers do as recorded in verse 45?

____

____

____

An amazing thing happens when others' needs become more important than our own–a family is formed; unity is achieved; and the body functions in the way it is intended. God has known this all along, and this is why he gave the body of Christ a wardrobe of generosity to wear.

Another way we can extend generosity is through our speech. Verse 29 says, "Do not let any unwholesome talk come out of your mouths, but only what is helpful for building others up according to their needs, that it may benefit those who listen." The apostle James, Christ's half-brother, warned believers in James 3:6 that the tongue "is a fire, a world of evil among the parts of the body. . . . corrupts

9. Ibid.

the whole person, sets the whole course of his life on fire, and is itself set on fire by hell." If left in the hands of the enemy, our tongues and our speech can become dangerous weapons–weapons used to divide the body of Christ instead of unite it.

With that in mind, write David's prayer in Psalms 141:3.

I pray that prayer a lot. Unfortunately, I do not pray it enough. At times, criticism slips from the doors of my lips, igniting a fire that can devour my brothers and sisters in Christ. I know that criticism is not helpful. It does nothing to build others up, nor does it benefit those who listen to it. All criticism does is make me feel better about myself.

Jesus said in his Sermon on the Mount in Matthew 5:7, "Blessed are the merciful, for they will be shown mercy." Mercy and criticism cannot coexist. Mercy is withholding from someone punishment (or criticism) which they rightly deserve. Mercy is what God gives us. And in actuality, mercy is the cure for criticism.

The Holy Spirit, who dwells within each member of the body of Christ, feels right at home when a wardrobe of honesty, love, generosity, and mercy adorn believers. But when we slip into the garments of the old self, Paul warns us in verse 30 that we run the risk of grieving the Holy Spirit.

Read Ephesians 4:31. Do the sins mentioned in this verse involve our relationship with God or our relationship with other people?

Why do you think the Holy Spirit would be grieved by these sins?

____

____

____

The whole intent of Ephesians 4 is to remind Christians that we are indeed *one* body. We are unified, and we need each other in order to grow into the full measure of Christ. Since the Holy Spirit lives within us and unifies us, he is grieved when we allow our emotions to separate us from each other.

Read Ephesians 4:32. To keep our emotions from separating us, Paul instructs us to do three things. What are they?

____

____

____

In the final verse of Ephesians 4, Paul lists some final characteristics that adorn the wardrobe of the body of Christ. In addition to honesty, love, generosity and mercy, believers are given kindness, compassion, and forgiveness to wear. Each one of these attributes assists us in maintaining unity within the body.

If I had never studied the movie *13 Going on 30*, I would not have recognized the change in Jenna's wardrobe. I'm not much of a fashion guru, so it's not surprising that such a thing would escape my attention. But there is someone who examines our spiritual wardrobe, and according to Hebrews 4:13, "nothing in all creation is hidden from God's sight. Everything is uncovered and laid bare before the eyes of him to whom we must give account."

With that verse in mind, write a note to the Lord below asking him what he sees when he examines your spiritual wardrobe. In recent months, has he noticed a change? Does he see you adorned in the complete wardrobe of your new self? Or are there articles of your old self that still feel more comfortable? Tell him what you desire he see when he looks at you.

Prayer—*Lord, when Adam and Eve recognized their sin in the garden, it was you who clothed them. You have longed to clothe your people ever since, not with the skin of animals, but with the wardrobe of a new self. Clothe me, I pray, from head to toe in this beautiful garment, and in so doing, make me a beautiful bride for Christ.*

HIS RUNAWAY BRIDE

Ephesians 5

VOW: ". . . and the two shall become one flesh. This is a profound mystery–but I am talking about Christ and the church."	**Ephesians 5:31–32**

Day 1: Walking in Love

Read Ephesians 5:1–7.

Maggie's athleticism necessitates her need for running shoes. The boxing gloves she wears and the punching bag she strikes are evidence of that. But Ike Graham's column in USA Today *suggests her Adidas's are used for other, more offensive purposes. She'd like to offend him; in fact, she'd prefer his face to the punching bag she currently pummels.*

Ike Graham is a coward, who hides behind words and initiates his altercations through slander. So any attempt at physical harm would be of little consequence to him and would only support his claims that Maggie Carpenter is a man-eater. No, she has to think of another way to accost the

New York reporter who has fabricated such horrible lies about her and printed them for all the world to read.

With one final left hook to the punching bag, Maggie rips off her gloves, tears the odious article from the wall, straddles her desk chair and begins typing. This runaway bride is not running from Mr. Graham's accusations. She will confront his editor head-on, disclosing his gross misrepresentation of the facts. And hopefully, she'll show this New York City reporter that her running shoes leave tread marks, not on the altar or the aisle, but this time, all over his column.

Movie Mania

To better understand this study of Ephesians 5, watch *Runaway Bride* and consider the following questions:

- Does Ike discover the real reason Maggie runs from love and commitment?
- Why does Maggie run from love and commitment?

Read Ephesians 5:25. In this passage, the relationship of Christ and the church is compared to what earthly relationship?

In Ephesians 4, Paul uses the example of a body to illustrate our relationship to Christ and to one another. In Ephesians 5, he uses the relationship of a husband and wife to parallel our union with Christ.

The marriage of the Lamb will not occur until sometime in the future (Revelation 19), but until that time, Christ doesn't want his bride getting cold feet. So he instructed Paul to write Ephesians 5 in order to keep us from being like Maggie Carpenter and running away.

He can't believe it. He's lost his column, his job, his credence in the journalistic community, and now, after a few brief questions at Curl Up and Dye, now he's lost his hair. And all because of her–the man-eater, the nefarious seductress, the runaway bride, Maggie Carpenter. As Ike sits across the table from her, listening to her father's banter regarding the financial expense he's incurred as a result of his daughter's cold feet, Ike feels certain he can expose her for the man-eater he thinks she is. Her fiancé sits to her left, coaching her with directives that she keep her eye on the ball. What kind of whacked-out family is this anyway?

Bob, Maggie's next victim, looks at Ike and explains his use of sports psychology to allay Maggie's fear of commitment. That will no doubt work, if in fact Maggie's veil converts to a helmet and the altar suddenly develops goal posts. Naïve little Bob, he actually thinks he has a chance to win this little game. Ike is certain the poor schmuck will be heading to the end zone alone.

In order to keep his notorious, runaway bride focused on the altar, fourth fiancé, Bob Kelly, utilizes sports psychology on Maggie and asks her to visualize the end zone (a.k.a. the altar). The apostle Paul went for a similar approach. In Ephesians 5, he encouraged the bride of Christ to focus on five things: walking in love, walking in the light, walking wisely, walking beneath protection, and walking beneath the cleansing power of the Word. For a potential runaway bride, such encouragement to walk could have resulted in hazardous outcomes. But the direction of this walking leads Christ's bride down the aisle and to the altar. So, as we study Ephesians 5, visualize the altar, and keep walking!

Read Ephesians 5:1–2. In this passage, Paul instructs the bride of Christ to do two things. What are they?

It is apparent to Ike that Bob's sports psychology knows no bounds. Just days before their wedding, Bob is still holding firmly to his method of coercion. This time, Maggie isn't keeping her eye on the ball. This time, she is the ball, spiraling down the aisle with Ike standing in as her wide receiver. Slowly she inches toward him, following Bob's instructions, maintaining eye contact, remaining focused–until finally, she reaches him.

In his attempts to "coach" his bride down the aisle, Bob Kelly conducts a "practice" wedding for Maggie so she can visualize the ceremony. In this scene of the movie at Hale Methodist Church, Bob tells Maggie to visualize herself as a football, spiraling down the aisle toward the hands of her awaiting groom.[1] Maggie has to imitate a pigskin ball in order to reach the altar, but in Ephesians 5, Paul wants the Savior's bride (the church) to imitate God on her way down the aisle.

According to 1 John 4:16, God is love. Paul tells us in 1 Corinthians 13 that love is patient and kind. It does not envy or boast. It is not proud or self-seeking. And everything love is, God is. He is patient and kind. He does not envy or boast. He is not proud or self-seeking. He is love, and we are most like him when we live a life of love.

The *New American Standard Bible* version of Ephesians 5:2 translates the verb "live" as "walk" and thus reads "walk in love." Therefore, we emulate God when we walk in love.

1. Josann McGibbon and Sara Parriott, "How Long Has This Been Going On?" *Runaway Bride.* DVD. Directed by Garry Marshall. Hollywood, CA: Paramount Pictures, 1999.

What do you think it means to walk in love?

____

____

____

Christ was not the only one who chose a bride. In Exodus 19, God chooses the entire nation of Israel to be his bride. And the first thing God did afterward was give her the Ten Commandments.

Read Exodus 20:3–5. What were the first two commandments God gave his new bride?

____

____

Read Jeremiah 2:1–5. Did God's bride follow his commands?

____

____

The apostle John says in 2 John 1:6 that we should walk in love. He also defines love as walking in obedience to God's commands. Jesus says in John 14:15, "If you love me, you will obey what I command." Therefore, one way to walk in love is to walk in obedience to God's commands.

In Ephesians 5:3–7, the Lord gives the Ephesians an array of commands. List a few of them below.

____

____

____

Compare verses 3 and 5 of Ephesians 5.

What three characteristics are repeated in these verses?

____

____

____

In verse 5, what does Paul call a person who possesses such characteristics?

____

____

____

Walking in love is definitely characterized by obedience. And Paul wrote verses 3–7 of Ephesians 5 in hopes that the Ephesians would obey all of God's commands. But obedience is just one aspect of love. The other aspect is focus. You see, walking in love is about making our groom the focal point of our lives. Idolatry was always such a distraction for the Israelites because it distracted them from their focus. On their way down the aisle, they forgot whom they loved. They took their eyes off their awaiting groom and sought affection elsewhere.

When I walked down the aisle on my wedding day, I remember looking into the crowd of well-wishers and seeing friends and family that I hadn't seen in years. They were all there, cheering me on. I was smiling and nodding and a bit distracted by all of them. I didn't stop walking, but I regret the fact that I took my eyes off my groom. Because as I walked down the aisle, he stood at the end, waiting for me, his eyes and his smile along with his look of devotion reserved only for me. I was his focus. No one else mattered. And I almost missed the sight of his sincere gaze because for a moment, my focus was elsewhere.

Immorality, impurity, and greed result when we, like the Israelites, allow our focus to wander elsewhere as we take our eyes off our groom and begin to idolize things or people around us. Sometimes our focus isn't even on outward things, sometimes our focus is inward. And we become the object of our own affections. Whether our attention is directed within or without, either way, any consuming focus apart from a focus on God is idolatry.

Idolatry and disobedience will always keep us from walking in love. But living with the awareness that we are on a journey and at the end of the aisle, our groom awaits, keeps us focused. That mindset allows us to maintain eye contact, to respond in obedience, and to walk down the aisle in love.

What are some ways you maintain eye contact with your heavenly groom? How do you focus solely upon the Lord?

___

___

___

___

___

___

___

___

___

___

___

Prayer—*Lord, my physical eyes have never seen you. But my spiritual eyes have. They've seen you walking among the lampstands through John's vision in Revelation 1:13–16. I used to read that chapter a lot, until I had you memorized. Until I was able to see you just as clearly as the apostle John had. Until I saw for myself your long robe with your golden sash draped around your chest. Your white woolen hair and your eyes ablaze like fire. That is who you are to me. Lord, let that vision of you remain in the forefront of my mind. Let it be my all-consuming focus. Let* you *be my all consuming focus. And from that focus, let obedience flow.*

Day 2: Walking in the Light

Read Ephesians 5:8–14.

How does Christ describe himself in John 8:12?

Read Ephesians 5:8. How are we described in this verse?

Read Ephesians 5:8–14. Paul tells us to do three things in this passage. What are they? (Hint: they're found in verses 8, 10, and 11.)

We are light by association, meaning that we enjoy the benefits of light and truth because we are betrothed to the one who is light and truth. Since we are no longer in darkness, Paul tells the bride of Christ to do three things: walk (or live) as children of light, find out what pleases the Lord, and expose the fruitless deeds of darkness.

Read John 3:19–21. Why would people love darkness?

Walking in the light requires honesty, honesty with ourselves and with our groom. In Ephesians 5:8, where Paul encourages us to walk as children of light, he is really asking us to walk in the light so that our deeds can be plainly exposed. So that there is nothing hidden between God and us. When we walk according to the truth of God's Word, then we have no reason to hide in darkness, for our deeds are pleasing to the Lord.

Review Ephesians 5:9. When we walk in the light, what kind of fruit do we produce?

In Ephesians 5:10, Paul commissions the Savior's bride to find out what pleases her groom, and according to John 15:8, God is glorified when we bear much fruit. Therefore, our groom is pleased when we cling to his truth and bear fruit that glorifies him. Fruit like goodness, righteousness, and truth give honor to God.

Light not only produces fruit and exposes the motives and intentions of the bride's heart, it also exposes evil. That is why Paul told the Savior's bride to "have nothing to do with the fruitless deeds of darkness, but rather expose them."[2]

Why do you think Christ would want his bride to expose evil?

____

____

____

In order to understand the heart of the groom, it is helpful to read the prayer he prayed for his church on the night he was betrayed. In this prayer, he petitions the Father for many things on behalf of his bride. But there is one thing that stands out.

Read John 17:15. What does Christ ask his Father to do in this verse?

____

____

____

In the film *Runaway Bride,* when Bob Kelly first meets Ike Graham, he doesn't initially see Ike as a threat to his relationship with Maggie. Likewise, Maggie doesn't see Ike as a threat to her relationship with Bob. In the beginning, Ike is merely a nuisance who has come to annoy them in the weeks prior to their wedding. But as

2. Ephesians 5:11.

time goes by, Ike becomes more than a nuisance. He becomes a stumbling block, stealing the bride's focus and eventually, altering the course of Bob and Maggie's relationship.

Sin has the same potential in our relationship with the Lord. While the enemy is incapable of snatching us out of our Savior's hands (John 10:28), he can still use sin to distract us and distance us from our groom.

In order to keep us from being deceived by the enemy, in John 17:15, Christ asks God the Father to protect us from the evil one. And one way we allow God to protect us is by walking in the light. Walking in the light merely means we allow God to expose the works of darkness in our lives. It means we allow God to identify stumbling blocks or habits that steal our focus away from him. When we walk in the light and become aware of our sin, then we are better able to protect our relationship with the Lord.

Has God ever exposed sin in your life? If so, after being made aware of that sin, how were you better able to protect your relationship with the Lord?

____

____

____

____

____

____

I don't frequently fall into many obvious sins like lying or theft. No, the more I mature in Christ, the more I realize how subtle my sins become. Currently, the sin I identify most often is the sin of excess–too much food, too much rest, too much TV. A year ago I was even convicted of too much reading.

As you may have noticed, I'm a bit of a sap. I love romance novels. And even though I only read Christian romance, I've found that when it comes to that area of my life, I fall into excess. In fact last year, I was standing in the library with my family, my arms laden with books for a week's worth of reading, when God enlightened me to my sin. He said something to the effect of, "Enough is enough, go put those books back." And I knew instantly that I had just stumbled into the light. My sin was exposed. And I had a choice. Either please God and put the books back, or please myself and keep reading.

It wasn't easy, but I put the books back and I've been aware of my weakness ever since. I haven't stopped reading, but I have begun to read in moderation now. And I'm thankful that God's light exposed my sin. His correction has kept me from exalting reading above him. Because whether it's reading or eating or watching too much TV–anything I do in excess steals my focus and hinders my relationship with the Lord.

Prayer–*Lord, I want to protect my relationship with you above all else. Please help me walk every day in your light. Expose my sins, and let nothing steal my focus away from you.*

Day 3: Walking Wisely

Read Ephesians 5:15–20.

Something is wrong. Maggie can tell by Peggy's curt exodus that things have not gone well with Ike. He made his grand entrance only moments ago, strolling through the crowd of softball spectators. Climbing the bleachers, he arrogantly parked himself right beside Peggy, managing to upset her in less than three minutes. That is a record, even for him. Irritating man.

What did he say to make Maggie's best friend take off like that? Peggy didn't even stop long enough to give Maggie a proper good-bye.

Movie Trivia Question

- In the stands, Ike tells Maggie the reason for Peggy's departure. What is the reason?

In Day 1 we were admonished by our Ephesians study to walk in love. In Day 2, we were encouraged to walk in the light, and today we will be challenged to walk wisely. But why do we need to walk wisely, and better yet, how do we do it?

Read Ephesians 5:15–16. According to verse 16, why do we need to walk wisely?

____

____

____

Peggy pours the contents of her Styrofoam cup into her favorite coffee mug. She grabs her drink and settles in the stylist chair to continue her heart-to-heart with Maggie. Maggie squirms in the adjacent seat and casually threatens suicide. Apparently, Maggie isn't responding well to the conversation.

How could Peggy say it without further offense? How can she explain Maggie's affect on people? How could she tell her the truth? Maggie is a flirt–a big flirt, but not an ostentatious one. More of a subtle, mysterious flirt whose ambiguity leaves men longing for more. She affects people–especially men–with her presence. And the crazy thing is that Maggie is unaware of it all.

Walking wisely is all about awareness. By commissioning us to walk wisely, God is merely asking us to be aware–be aware of him; our surroundings; ourselves, including our strengths and our weaknesses. We are to be aware of everything because we are walking in evil times.

In the film, Maggie has no hostile motives. She has no evil intent. And yet she offends her best friend because she is unaware of her own self. She is unaware of her effect on others–unaware of the fact that her behavior often makes people feel bad.

Wisdom is awareness. And in our passage today, Paul gives us four things that we, as Christians, should be aware of.

What should we be aware of according to Ephesians 5:17?

When I first began growing in my relationship with the Lord, one thing I had to learn was that God had an opinion about every area of my life. In other words, he had his own will for the direction I should take in life. Once I was aware of this concept, the next thing I had to learn was the discipline to seek him in order to truly know his will.

In verse 17, Paul merely encourages us to pursue God's will for our lives. He wants us to be aware that God has a plan and a will for each of us. In verse 18, Paul seeks to inform us of the method by which we discover God's will.

Read Ephesians 5:18.

What are we not supposed to do? And why?

___

___

___

What are we supposed to do?

___

___

___

An excess of alcohol hinders our awareness. It desensitizes us to our surroundings, rendering us naïve and helpless. But the Spirit of God guides us into all truth, making us cognizant of both the physical and spiritual realms (see John 16:13). When we're aware of our physical and spiritual surroundings, then we're better able to acknowledge God's presence in every area of life. And as we acknowledge his presence, we're able to discover his will.

What are we encouraged to do in Ephesians 5:19–20?

___

___

___

By speaking spiritual songs, hymns, and psalms to others, we heighten our awareness of spiritual matters. We keep the spirit realm in the forefront of our minds. And we enable others to do the same. By singing to God and offering him our thanksgiving, we acknowledge his goodness to us. We become aware of his kindness and generosity.

Walking in wisdom is walking in awareness–an awareness that God has a will for our lives. An awareness of God's Holy Spirit sent to guide us into all truth. An awareness of the spirit realm as we speak forth God's praises to other believers. And, finally, walking in wisdom is an awareness of God's goodness to us. Being aware of these four things enables us to walk in wisdom on our journey down the aisle.

What will you be most aware of this week, and why? Check one and explain your answer.

- ☐ aware God has a will for your life
- ☐ aware of God's Spirit guiding you into all truth
- ☐ aware of the spirit realm (by expressing spiritual thoughts to others)
- ☐ aware of God's goodness

____

____

____

____

____

____

Day 4: Walking beneath Protection

Read Ephesians 5:21–24.

The verses we will study today compare two relationships. Read Ephesians 5:21–24.

☐ What two relationships are compared in these verses?

____

____

____

____

☐ What is the wife (and the church) commissioned to do in this passage?

____

____

____

____

____

☐ Read Ephesians 5:25. According to this verse, what are husbands commissioned to do concerning their wives?

____

____

____

____

☐ Read 1 Corinthians 13:7 and fill in the blank.

"(Love) It always ____________________, always trusts, always hopes, always perseveres."

Christ always intended for his bride to be protected. That is why he made himself the head of the church. From the beginning of time,

God intended for women to walk beneath the protection of men. In the Old Testament, God held men to a higher standard of accountability because they were in a position of leadership. For example, if a man made a hasty, rash vow to the Lord, then he was required to fulfill it. (This was the case with Jephthah in Judges 11.) But if a woman made an irresponsible vow to the Lord, then her husband or father could nullify that vow and the Lord would release her from it (Numbers 30:1–8). The woman's husband or father represented her protective authority, protecting her not only from others, but also from herself.

In Ephesians 5:21–24, both Christ and husbands represent protective authority. But it is the church's choice, as well as the woman's choice, as to whether or not we will walk beneath that protective authority.

Read Romans 13:1. What does Paul say about authority in the second part of this verse?

____

____

____

____

____

Read Romans 13:2. According to this verse, when we rebel against authority, against whom are we ultimately rebelling?

____

____

____

____

Read Ephesians 5:21. When we choose to submit to authority, to whom are we really submitting?

Movie Trivia Question

- In Day 3, we studied the scene where Peggy and Maggie are having a heart-to-heart talk at Curl Up & Dye. At the conclusion of this scene, what does Peggy ask Maggie to do?

In this lesson on submission, I must issue a caveat. Please know that God intends for us to submit to authority, but not to abuse. So seek God's guidance and allow the Holy Spirit to lead you in determining what authority is God-given and what authority is merely an abuse of power.

During the filming of *Runaway Bride,* director Garry Marshall found himself in search of an ending for the scene at Curl Up & Dye. The script had not provided him with one, so like all brilliant directors, he watched his actors, observing their behavior on and off the set. He discovered his ending when he saw Julia Roberts entertaining his twin granddaughters.

On their visit to the set one day, Garry Marshall's three-year-old granddaughters were mesmerized by Roberts' facial expressions. Julia Roberts made funny faces in order to make them laugh and one face was the duckbill platypus. Upon seeing it, Garry Marshall knew he had to include it in the movie.

At first, Roberts was opposed to the idea, stating it could ruin her career, but eventually she assented, granting Marshall his request. In the movie, Roberts makes the platypus face and then says, "This is so humiliating."[3] According to Garry Marshall, her comment was addressed to him, not toward Peggy.[4]

Submission to authority reveals two things about a relationship. It reveals *trust* and *respect.* Though Julia Roberts was not immediately fond of the idea of the Duckbill Platypus, she eventually came around. Her submission to Marshall's authority revealed a relationship of trust and respect.

I've been called to submit to authority that I neither trusted nor respected. One such instance was when I was working full-time as a social worker. I did not respect my supervisor as I should have and during a meeting one day she gave me yet another instruction regarding my already enormous case load. I made a rather rebellious remark in front of everyone and later found myself in a disciplinary meeting with my boss and another supervisor (not my finest moment!).

While there may not have been trust and respect in my relationship with my supervisor, my actions ultimately revealed that there was not trust and respect in my relationship with the Lord. My rebellion against my boss's authority not only meant I didn't trust her, it ultimately meant I didn't trust God.

Five years later, after losing contact with that woman and moving two thousand miles away, the Lord convicted me of my rebellion. (I'm not really sure what the statute of limitation is for insubor-

3. McGibbon and Parriott, "Profoundly and Irreversibly Screwed Up." *Runaway Bride.* DVD.
4. Ibid.

dination, but in God's economy five years obviously does nothing to absolve an unrepentant offense.) The Lord instructed me to track her down, call her, and ask her forgiveness. After much whining on my part, I finally made the phone call. My former supervisor was surprised to receive my call, but she was gracious enough to accept my apology.

It required a great deal of humiliation on my part, but I did what God instructed me to do. I submitted to the Lord's will because I had wronged my former supervisor and I needed to apologize. And I'm so thankful I did, because that apology allowed for greater trust and respect in my relationship with the Lord. Ephesians 5:21 tells us to "submit to one another out of reverence for Christ." We will all inevitably be placed under authority that we question, but submission to that authority out of reverence for Christ evidences a heart that truly trusts God.

Read Hebrews 13:17. How does this verse describe our leaders?

____

____

____

John 17 records Christ's prayer to the Father regarding the church. In verses 6–8, Jesus himself gives an account for his actions toward his bride. He let the Father know he had given the church the words he had been instructed to give them.

God will one day call all those in authority to give an account for their actions. As Christ gave an account for the way he protected the church, so husbands will give an account for the way they protect their wives. And one day, every wife, including the bride of Christ, will have to give an account as to whether or not she walked beneath the protection of that authority.

Describe the authority to whom God has called you to submit. (This authority may come in the form of a husband or a supervisor or a pastor or spiritual mentor.) Cite an example where you demonstrated trust and respect in your relationship with the Lord by submitting to this authority.

Prayer—*Lord, help me come to the point where I recognize my need for your protection. Thank you that you offer me protection through the authority you've placed over me. Help me trust you enough to walk beneath the protection of that authority.*

Day 5: Walking beneath the Cleansing Power of the Word

Read Ephesians 5:25–33.

The Fed-Ex truck is the only available means of transportation. Maggie jumps aboard and stands like a porcelain statue in the doorway, her white dress blowing in the wind. The truck carries her away from the crowd of reporters, all gawking at her. Their knowing looks and contemptuous smirks tell her they knew she'd run. They know her better than she knows herself.

But she isn't running from them. She is running from Ike. She just hasn't considered the possibility that he'd run after her. Guilt pierces her heart as she watches him, his tie flapping in the wind as his legs reach top speed. His Armani suit and designer shoes make for poor running attire. But he is persistent in his pursuit. And with each winded breath, her name is uttered from his lips.

Read Ephesians 5:25. How are husbands instructed to love their wives?

____

____

Paul continues his analogy comparing Christ's relationship to the church with the marriage relationship. And in so doing, Paul offers his readers a dual teaching. One teaching instructs husbands how to love their wives, while the other teaching reveals Christ's unfettered love for his bride. For today's study, we will examine Christ's love for his bride.

According to Ephesians 5:25, what did Christ's love for the church cause him to do?

____

____

Christ's love for his bride is made evident by the fact that he gave himself up for her. However, his sacrifice did more than just proclaim his love. He had another reason for doing what he did.

Ike's apartment is much homier than Maggie would have imagined. His friendly cat, Italics, has warmed up to her nicely. Maggie only hopes Italics's owner will do the same.

The door opens, and Maggie remains silent, her scripted words reverberating in her head. Ike places his overcoat in the closet and sees Maggie's reflection in the mirror. The surprise on his face is quickly replaced by a look of disdain. She had expected as much.

His distant manner indicates she has little time to explain her actions. But she owes him this much. She owes him an explanation. He has to know the reason she ran.

Once he sits on the porch steps, she knows he's granted her his undivided attention. So she begins to explain. The truth is that she'd always tried to be who others wanted her to be, assuming their likes and dislikes, taking on their traits and characteristics. She'd desired to give her grooms what she thought they wanted. Gill, Brian, George, Bob–they'd all seen Maggie in their own way, but they'd never seen the real Maggie. They were in love with an image. An image Maggie had portrayed to them. But that image had robbed Maggie of her true identity. And she didn't know who she really was anymore. But Ike knows the real Maggie. He'd always known the real Maggie, and that realization had frightened her, frightened her enough to make her run.

Read Ephesians 5:26. Why did Christ give himself up for his bride?

____

____

____

Christ knows his bride. He knows us for who we really are. He sees through the image of holiness we try to portray. He sees past our plastic smiles and our cheerful fronts. He sees us; he knows us, and he recognizes our need for holiness.

How do you feel, knowing that Christ sees you for who you truly are, and yet, loves you still?

____

____

____

____

____

Our Groom has an amazing kind of love. He not only sees us and loves us for who we are, he sees us and loves us for who we will be. He loves us with the intent of making us holy. And according to verse 26, he assumes complete responsibility for this transformation process.

Reread Ephesians 5:26, how does Christ cleanse us and make us holy?

Many of us understand that Christ's blood cleanses us and provides us salvation. But here verse 26 tells us that Christ himself washes us (the church) and makes us holy through his word (the doctrines and promises of God revealed and taught in the Bible[5]). The theological term for Christ making us holy is "sanctification," and it refers to the act of setting apart something for a sacred use. Therefore, as the bride of Christ, we are set apart for him. Our lives are being made holy through him and for him. First, Christ assumes responsibility for saving us and then he assumes responsibility for sanctifying us.

Read Ephesians 5:27. Why did Christ want to sanctify his bride?

Read Ephesians 5:31–32. Why would it be important for the bride of Christ to be holy and blameless?

---

5. Spiros Zodhiates, *The Complete Word Study Dictionary: New Testament* (Chattanooga, TN: AMG Publishers, 1992), #4487 *rheâma,* 1262–63.

Christ left everything in order to unite himself with his bride, the church. He left his heavenly abode and even endured his Father's rejection on the cross when he carried the sins of his bride. He went to great lengths to make her holy because he knew he could not be united with unrighteousness. He knew according to 2 Corinthians 6:14, that he could not be unequally yoked.

So therefore, he takes his bride and washes her in the Word in order to make her holy and blameless. He does all of this to make her the bride he deserves to have standing by his side.

What are some ways that we, as the bride of Christ, can allow our Groom to wash us in his Word?

____

____

____

____

A bride in love always wants to be pure for her groom. But while we alone can never make ourselves holy and blameless, we can lean into Christ's cleansing process by walking every day with God's Word in our hearts, comparing our actions and feelings against the Word of God.

Prayer—*Lord, thank you that you go to such great lengths to make me pure. Help me allow your cleansing Word access to every area of my life. Because more than anything I want to stand by your side as a holy and blameless bride.*

HIS RESOLUTE BRIDE

Ephesians 6

VOW: "Therefore put on the full armor of God, so that when the day of evil comes, you may be able to stand your ground . . ."	**Ephesians 6:13**

Day 1: Resolve to Be Unified

Read Ephesians 6:1–9.

While Ephesians 5 leaves the bride of Christ with visions of her wedding day, Ephesians 6 has her dressed in army fatigues and combat boots. Seems a rather unsavory depiction, unless, of course, the fatigues are designer and the boots are Prada®.

In the 2003 best-selling novel, *The Devil Wears Prada*, author Lauren Weisberger serves up a conflict of emotion in her story of an egomaniacal supervisor and her indentured administrative assistant. Had Weisberger's book been just another employer versus employee chronicle, then it may not have garnered much interest. But drawing from her own personal experience at *Vogue,* Weisberger sets her interoffice struggle amid the glamour of the high world of fashion.

Ephesians 6 gives us a glimpse into the conflict occurring within the spirit realm. In this final chapter of Ephesians, we will learn God's plan for warfare and the role the bride of Christ plays in this spiritual battle against the enemy. But before we arm for war, Paul thought it important to establish some rules within the enlisted ranks.

Read Ephesians 6:1–9. How many times is the word "obey" repeated in this passage?

____

Who is to obey whom as stated in these verses?

____

____

Reread verses 4 and 9. What are those in authority required to do?

____

____

____

____

In Ephesians 6, Paul is directly addressing the church. Verses 1–9 teach members of the body how to operate within their God-given roles. While the church consists of a variety of people, each in varying ranks of authority, everyone within the church unites to become a spiritual warrior.

In your opinion, what occurs when God's people do not show respect and obedience within their God-given roles?

____

____

____

After graduating from Cornell University in 1999, Lauren Weisberger submitted a resume to Conde Nast Publications, *Vogue*'s parent company. They offered her a position, and she soon found herself in the role of administrative assistant to the most powerful woman in fashion, Anna Wintour. The British-born Wintour has been *Vogue*'s editor in chief since 1988 and has become a stylish icon, known throughout the fashion industry for her waif-like figure, her aloof deportment, and her decisive persona.

Weisberger's stint as Anna Wintour's assistant lasted a little less than a year, but it left an impression on the young writer. Critics claim Weisberger fashioned her main character, the devilish Miranda Priestly, after her former boss, Wintour. Though Weisberger adamantly denies the accusation, those in the fashion industry have argued otherwise.

Every good writer knows that the main ingredient for a wonderful plot is conflict. Conflict, conflict, conflict–it produces great drama. In *The Devil Wears Prada,* author Lauren Weisberger serves audiences a healthy portion of it. But when it occurs within the ranks of Christ's unified bride, it can have devastating consequences. Therefore, to effectively wage war against the enemy, we must resolve to be unified. Unity on the battlefield is of the utmost importance.

Paul knew that a unified army was an effective army. Therefore, from the outset of Ephesians 6, he establishes a code of conduct for believers in order to promote unity within the body of Christ. He instructs those in authority to be kind and respectful of their subordinates. Likewise slaves and children are commissioned to honor and obey their masters and parents. Not out of obligatory duty, but out of love for the Lord.

One of the primary objectives of the enemy is to disrupt unity within the body of Christ. According to Ephesians 4:26–27, what is one way the enemy can achieve this?

Anything that distracts us from the battle can make us ineffective warriors. Since there is a chain of command within the body of Christ, relationships within the body can become tenuous if void of honor and respect. Oftentimes, other brothers and sisters in Christ fail to show us honor and respect and therefore offend us and make us angry. As a result, the enemy can gain a foothold, and for a moment, we can believe that our true enemy are our fellow soldiers.

Have you ever mistaken a fellow Christian for an enemy? I know I have, but what are some ways that we, as the body of Christ, can resolve to be unified?

When I am hurt or angered by a fellow believer, I do two things. First, I'm reminded of the King James translation of Psalm 119:165. It reads, "Great peace have they which love thy law: and nothing shall offend them." As a result of this verse, I examine the offense and try to determine if my own insecurities have caused me to become offended–because offense is a deceptive symptom of pride. If I'm easily offended, then the problem is not with my brother or sister in Christ, the problem is with me.

The second thing I do when conflict occurs is remember Proverbs 19:11, "A man's wisdom gives him patience; it is to his glory to overlook an offense." If my own insecurities have not incited the offense, and I've truly been wronged, then I'm left with a decision. Either hold fast to my anger and relish the right to be angry, or vent my anger for a day and then at nightfall, choose to overlook the offense.

Just this past week, one of my sisters in Christ said some very hurtful things to me. She didn't do it out of malice, but rather out of immaturity, and I knew this, but it still hurt deeply. After the altercation, I read Proverbs 19:11 and by the grace of God, I made the decision to overlook the offense. I made the choice to forgive. As a sign of this forgiveness, I called her and told her I loved her no matter what. And when I hung up, I felt free.

On May 23, 2006, the woman who was supposedly the inspiration for Weisberger's antagonist in the book, *The Devil Wears Prada*, bravely entered the Paris Theatre in New York City to view the premiere of the movie. Accompanied by her daughter Bee Shaffer and acquaintance Shelby Bryan, Anna Wintour made her grand entrance amid wagging tongues and gossip reporters. But she garnered their respect when observers noticed her outfit's designer label. It was Prada®, of course.[1]

1. "Movie Maven (Anna Wintour at the movie premiere)," *Women's Wear Daily*, May 25, 2006, http://www.highbeam.com/doc/1G1-146549594.html.

When interviewed by Barbara Walters in December of 2006, Wintour said she thought the film was "really entertaining." She also stated that "anything that makes fashion entertaining and glamorous and interesting is wonderful for our industry. So I was 100 percent behind it."[2]

Prayer—*Lord, give me eyes to see the spiritual battle that is taking place. Let me not be distracted by the disputes I may have with other members of the body of Christ. Let me look beyond those things and forgive or ask forgiveness. Let me resolve to live in unity by refusing to allow the sun to go down on my wrath. And together, let your body unite to battle the real enemy.*

Day 2: Resolve to Be Strengthened

 **Read Ephesians 6:10–12.**

Movie Mania

To better understand this study of Ephesians 6, watch *The Devil Wears Prada* and consider the following questions:

- There are two conflicts going on in the movie. What are they?
- While surrounded by the world of fashion, does Andrea "Andy" Sachs stay true to her convictions?

2. Barbara Walters, "The 10 Most Fascinating People of 2006," December 12, 2006, http://abcnews.go.com/2020/story?id=2716887&page=3.

Andy's hair hangs like a limp dishrag around her pale face. As she steps from the elevator, her uneven layers chase her as she turns her head from side to side in search of the receptionist's desk. Pivoting to her left she walks through the sleek glass doors, dodging a moving rack of designer fashions. She approaches the receptionist's desk, completely unaware of the fact that her white oxford, purple pullover, and corduroy blazer identifies her as an interloper. She is an outsider, and everyone at Runway *is quick to recognize her as such. Everyone knows . . . except Andy.*

Read Ephesians 6:10–12. Observe verse 12 closely and fill in the blank below.

"For our _______________ is not against flesh and blood, but against the powers of this dark world and against the spiritual forces of evil in the heavenly realms."

Emily takes one look at Andy and knows immediately Human Resources has begun a "mission of mercy" campaign. If Runway*'s parent company, Elias-Clarke Publications, is suddenly taking an interest in the urchins of New York, then so be it, but she shouldn't have to suffer for their sympathetic heart sighs. The folks at Human Resources must be getting a good laugh over this one. Little Andy Sachs, donning her Wal-Mart apparel and sloppy haircut, has just entered a hostile environment. And as Emily ushers her down the halls of* Runway, *she is certain her coworkers will see a target on Andy's back.*

In the movie, there is something very endearing about Andy's initial naïveté. It's as if she's walking through *Runway,* excited about the opportunity for her first job, eager to meet any unknown challenges it may require. She's oblivious to the interoffice hostility and the demanding supervisor whose expectations are as high as her stilettos. Instead, Andy is just happy to be there and blissfully unaware of the reality of her situation.

I wonder if the Ephesian church enjoyed the same euphoric feeling before reading the conclusion to Paul's letter. His first five chapters are filled with instructions of God's love and their appropriate response to that love. So it's possible his words of endearment and instruction were received with an ample amount of idealism and naïveté.

But his final words to the church at Ephesus blatantly inform them of reality. They're walking in hostile territory, and therefore, they're in the midst of a struggle. And not just any struggle, a spiritual struggle.

In fact, the Greek word Paul uses is best translated "wrestle" and to the Ephesians, this term referred to a contest between two opponents. The winner had to pin his opponent on the ground, holding him down with his hands on his neck. In exchange for a victorious fight, the winner would receive credit for his victory, but most importantly, he would escape the punishment that befell the loser. Losers had their eyes gouged out.

Since a loss accounted for such a great penalty, it became utterly important that the Ephesians succeed in their struggle. Likewise, it's equally important that we succeed in our spiritual struggle.

Therefore, in Ephesians 6:10 Paul divulges the secret to winning this spiritual battle. What does he instruct us to do in this passage?

____

____

____

The term "be strong" is translated from the Greek word, *endunamoo,* meaning "to clothe one's self with strength as one puts on a garment."[3] This verb is in the passive voice, meaning it's a continual act. Since our strength comes from the Lord, we must resolve to be continually strengthened by him. We never cease in this

3. Kenneth S. Wuest, *Wuest's Word Studies from the Greek New Testament: Volume I* (Grand Rapids, MI: Wm. B. Eerdmans Publishing Company, 1973), 140.

process. We must continually allow ourselves to be wrapped within the garment of strength that only God can provide.

While walking the halls of *Runway*, Andy is judged for her apparel. Others view her as an easy target. But when we're engaged in our spiritual struggle, clothed in the strength of our Lord Jesus Christ, our enemy fails to find a bull's-eye on our backs.

How can we, as Christians, clothe ourselves in the strength of the Lord?

Well, I believe that before we can be strengthened, we must first recognize our need for strength. We must admit that we, like the Ephesians, are in the midst of a spiritual struggle–a spiritual struggle that we can't win. Therefore, we need God. We need his intervention and his strength, not just periodically, but continually, every day.

This awareness humbles me, compelling me to seek God on a continual basis. And while I'm with him, I request his protection through his garment of spiritual strength. It's a garment I can seek out every day and its designer never denies me the privilege of donning it. All I need do is ask.

Prayer–*Lord, thank you for giving me everything I need to survive this spiritual struggle. Help me resolve to be strengthened by you every day. For without you, there could be no victory.*

Day 3: Resolve to Stand Firm in the Truth

Read Ephesians 6:13–17.

Yesterday we received a fashion lesson. We discovered our need to clothe ourselves daily with God's strength. But we're not yet quite ready to walk the runway. First, we must learn the coordinating accessories that accompany our garment of strength. And most importantly, we must learn posture.

Andy lands the job. But she views it as a necessary evil, a lowly rung on the ladder to journalistic success. She won't be able to write that much, but once she pays her dues, she is certain she can secure a job at any publication in New York, namely, The New Yorker. *All she needs do is survive Miranda's curt dismissals, meet her impossible demands, and endure her demonic demeanor. And hopefully, after a year spent in purgatory, she'll escape unscathed with a letter of recommendation.*

Read Ephesians 6:13. What are we to put on?

___

___

___

After only a few days on the job, Andy follows her coworker, Nigel, into Miranda's office and watches as the poor little underlings responsible for the run-through bolt about the room pandering to one unpleasant Miranda Priestly. Miranda is on a roll today, doling out criticism for the designers attempting to please her. She seems to be particularly fixated on their incompetence and finds every opportunity to exploit it.

Andy is able to observe the scene before her in relative silence. She watches as Miranda peruses the articles of clothing, dismissing each as she goes. Miranda's foul mood is deteriorating quickly. Suddenly she comes across a most unpleasant dress with ruffles and scarlet tulle and a fake flower to boot. Andy thinks it hideous, but Miranda seems pleased. It isn't ostentatious enough on its own though, according to Miranda, it needs accessories. So Miranda's minion scurries about to procure two seemingly identical blue belts. No doubt that will go nicely with the flamboyant red and white ball of fluff.

Read Ephesians 14–17 and list the items that make up our spiritual ensemble.

____

____

____

What is the first item listed?

____

To Miranda, a belt was merely an accessory. But to a first-century soldier, it was an essential piece of armor. It was indispensable because it was the item upon which the rest of the armor was secured. All other parts of the armor were attached to the belt.

According to John 14:6, what is truth?

____

____

____

As Christians, our armor is held intact by truth. And that truth is found in Christ. Since the Bible reveals that Christ is our only means of salvation, then truth can be narrowed down to one essential certainty. Truth is the knowledge that God has given us eternal life through his Son, Jesus Christ. That is the truth upon which all other pieces of our armor are secured.

Therefore, in this postmodern era where truth is relative and religious tolerance is touted, it is essential that we bind ourselves with the belt of truth. It is critical that we never waver in our position, but rather assume the posture of a warrior who has resolved to stand firm in the truth of Jesus Christ.

Andy has every intention of following Nigel's initial directive to remain silent. But when the frantic designer holds up two blue belts, insisting they differ immensely, Andy makes the crucial mistake of snickering. A snicker–one careless, uncensored snicker–has escaped her lips. Suddenly, Miranda's weighty gaze falls on Andy. Oh dear, this isn't good.

According to Ephesians 6:13–14, what posture should we assume while donning our armor of God?

____

____

____

After the ill-fated snicker, Miranda gives the fashion-challenged Andy a lesson in macroeconomics. Shortly thereafter, Andy receives another scathing bout of criticism from Miranda. (This time, Andy's blunder is her failure to secure a flight for Miranda in the midst of a hurricane.) After these unfortunate encounters with the fashion queen, Andy makes some fashion changes. She seeks Nigel's advice and he outfits her in new apparel.

But while Andy's wardrobe benefits immensely from these alterations, Andy's new interest in all things fashionable brings about changes in her attitude and in her priorities in life. Her journalistic dreams are placed on hold while she immerses herself in her job, allowing Miranda's demands to dictate her life.

Movie Trivia Question

- Throughout the course of the movie, what internal change occurs in Andy's life? How does that change affect her relationship with her boyfriend and her closest friends?

During an interview, the movie's director, David Frankel, describes Andy's character saying, "she's on the path toward being someone who's made sacrifices so deep that they've transformed who she is."[4] Andy's mistake isn't her sudden interest in fashion. Her error comes when she makes continual sacrifices that keep her from being true to her original convictions. In other words, she fails to stand firm.

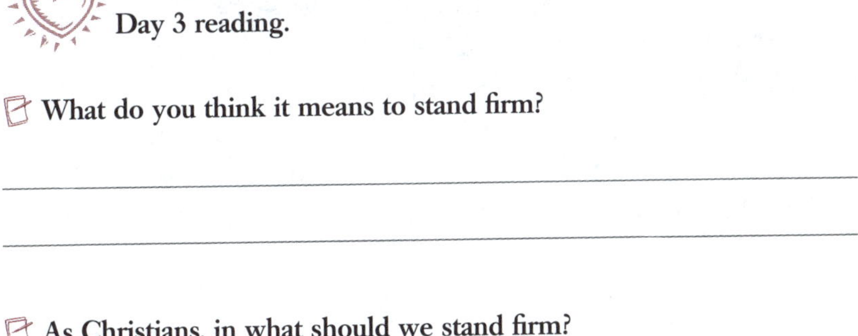

Answer the following questions as we begin to close out this Day 3 reading.

What do you think it means to stand firm?

____

____

As Christians, in what should we stand firm?

____

4. Aline Brosh McKenna, "The Trip to the Big Screen Featurette," *The Devil Wears Prada*. DVD. Directed by David Frankel (Beverly Hills, CA: Twentieth Century Fox, 2006.)

As Christians, we may rethink and alter certain aspects of our faith. In fact, I think that's a good thing. It shows maturity. The entire Protestant Reformation is mostly the result of one man who reconsidered his faith and altered his convictions accordingly. As a result, Christianity moved from a works-based religion to a faith founded upon salvation by grace through faith in Christ's work on the cross.

So with that in mind, I am open to the possibility of redefining my faith. For instance, there are doctrinal issues that I need to consider. For example, concerning doctrines such as eternal security, dispensationalism, and predestination–I was raised to believe a certain way about these doctrines but have since reevaluated my views, altering my opinion on some of them. There are interpretations of scripture that I grapple with and examine and consider and then reconsider. There are a lot of issues within my faith that I rethink and alter.

But there is one aspect of truth upon which I do not vacillate. There is one truth I do not question or reconsider. I can't, it's too important because it's the one truth upon which my faith is built. It is the truth that Jesus Christ's sacrifice on the cross covers my sins and allows me a relationship with the Lord.

This truth is nonnegotiable. It's not a truth we can question or reconsider. It is the primary truth in which we must stand firm. We should envelop ourselves in it and bind ourselves with it. So that when the enemy attacks, we're firm in our belief and confident of our standing with God. It is this primary truth upon which our faith is founded because it forms the basis of our relationship with the Lord.

Prayer–*Lord, sometimes I get so distracted by all the various beliefs within Christianity. Often doctrines become a hindrance to my faith because I'm so focused on them that I fail to stand firm in the simple truth of the gospel. So Lord, with that in mind, please renew my strength and enable me to stand firm in your truth.*

Day 4: Resolve to Communicate

Read Ephesians 6:18–20.

Andy is determined to support her best friend Lilly, so she arrives at the gallery to admire the art show Lilly has coordinated. During the art show, a misunderstanding occurs and Lilly accuses Andy of being unfaithful to her boyfriend, Nate. After Lilly's sharp rebuke, Andy has no desire to contend with Nate. So she makes her way to the door before he has the chance to berate her about her trip to Paris. As she flees the gallery, he pursues her, calling her name. Great, now she'll have to talk to him, and right now, she doesn't feel up to a conversation with her unhappy boyfriend.

This week we've been encouraged to be Christ's resolute bride. In Day 1, we resolved to be unified. In Day 2, we resolved to be strengthened. Yesterday we discovered that the enemy's assault against us requires that we resolve to stand firm in the truth, because the truth of Jesus Christ secures our relationship with the Lord. Today we'll resolve to protect that relationship through communication.

The enemy's attack against us is rooted in his desire to separate us from God. According to Romans 8:35–39 what can separate us from the love of God?

____

____

____

The truth is that nothing can separate us from the love of God. But the enemy isn't attacking God's love for us. He's attacking our love for God. Through the devil's deception, through adversity, and through life's failures and successes, we can easily become distracted with other things, and if we're not careful, we'll turn from our first love.

☐ In the introduction of our study, we discussed the Ephesians' long-term relationship with the Lord. What was the status of their relationship in Revelation 2:4?

☐ How can we keep from making the same mistake in our relationship with the Lord?

☐ Read Ephesians 6:18–20. In his closing comments to the Ephesians, what does Paul instruct them to do?

Nate stands on the sidewalk with Andy, her designer clothes and heavy eye shadow concealing the woman he'd fallen in love with. She now dresses differently, she thinks differently, and she acts differently. Her job at Runway *has launched her into a new hemisphere and he's been left behind.*

It is time he faced the truth. Andy has made her choice. She's repeatedly chosen Runway *and Miranda over him. Miranda now dictates Andy's time and decisions. In fact, Miranda even dictates Nate and Andy's relationship. It is time they both own up to that fact.*

They no longer communicate, and they no longer have anything in common. Her trip to Paris will give them the time apart they need–a separation, the prelude to a breakup. Nate stands there with Andy, the silence between them a mere challenge for one of them to recant. Neither says a word until Nate turns and walks away. As he makes his retreat, she calls his name.

He halts at her voice, quick to turn in her direction. He is met with silence, but he patiently awaits her words of reconciliation. The shrill sound of Andy's cell phone reaches his ears before any apology she might have offered. He knows who is calling, and so does Andy. Miranda. It is always Miranda.

Andy fumbles for her phone as she apologizes for the intrusion. Intent on taking the call, Andy begs Nate to wait while she talks to her boss. Nate, of course, has reached his limit. With the phone still ringing, he begins to walk away. But before he leaves, he turns to Andy with one final comment. "Ya' know, in case you were wondering, the person whose calls you always take, that's the relationship you're in. I hope you two are very happy together."[5]

Communication, it's the lifeline of a relationship. It's the secret to every great marriage. It's what keeps couples grounded and growing in the same direction. It's the tie that binds our hearts together, and it's the chord that unites our hearts with God.

Communication with the Lord is the basis of a relationship with him. It's what keeps the distractions of this world at bay, protecting our affections for our first love. I try to talk to God all the time–in the car, in the store, when I'm with my family, when I'm writing or speaking to an audience, or when I'm talking to a friend. There's this internal dialogue going on in my mind. I figure that God gave us the ability to multitask for a reason. So I try to do just that when it comes to prayer.

5. McKenna, "One of Them." *The Devil Wears Prada.* DVD.

Write 1 Thessalonians 5:17 below.

Continual prayer is an important component of my relationship with the Lord. However, there are moments in my relationship with him where everything takes a backseat and God receives my undivided attention. Sometimes those moments occur at my dining room table with a cup of coffee, my Bible, and my prayer journal. Other times, I escape to a park near my house where I enjoy the scenic view of tall pines encamped about a small lake. This is where I go to be alone with God and pray. This is my secret place.

Do you have a secret place where you go to talk to God? If so, explain how you feel about that place.

There's a peace that settles over me when I'm at my secret place. In fact, I'm here now, writing this final chapter. And I just love this place. I come here when life's good and happiness has overtaken me. I come here when the stress of life has choked the joy from me. And I seek refuge here when disappointment and failure assail me. I come here, not because it's a peaceful setting, but because it's where I go to commune with the Prince of Peace.

There's warfare that occurs when we talk to God. Paul informs us of that through his writings in Ephesians 6 and 2 Corinthians 10:4. But I think this offensive weapon of prayer isn't so much about the enemy's demise, as it is about our spiritual survival. We need prayer. Not just because it's a powerful weapon capable of demolishing strongholds, but because constant prayer reaffirms our relationship with the Lord. It reunites us with our first love. It keeps our relationship intact.

Isn't that the goal–an intimate relationship with the Lord? Our goal isn't to overcome the enemy; that's Christ's battle. Our goal is to communicate with our Creator, to stand firm and escape this life with the Lord as our first love.

Prayer–*Lord, I love you so much. I want my life to be one constant conversation with you. Help me to listen and respond to you. Help me share my heart with you, even when I've sinned. You are my best friend, Lord, so let nothing keep us from enjoying a lifetime of communication.*

Day 5: Resolve to Love with an Undying Love

Read Ephesians 6:21–24.

The sights of the city are like a movie reel flashing from one scene to another, but Andy pays little heed as the chauffeur speeds down the streets of Paris.

Her mind is elsewhere, recalling the scene she has just witnessed–the luncheon in which Miranda destroyed Nigel's dreams in order to further her own. Andy aches for Nigel. And she feels contempt for the woman by her side.

Miranda sits against the leather upholstery, her silence the shroud she wears to intimidate others. Andy has seen that cloak before, and she responds with equal stillness. Tension permeates the backseat. Miranda is the first to speak–her words prove that she is quite pleased with her deceitful accomplishment and that she considers her betrayal a mere business decision. Andy remains quiet, able to stomach Miranda's excuses until Miranda makes the painful comment that Andy reminds her of herself.

That comparison draws a swift response, and Andy denies that claim with disgust. She doesn't want to be like Miranda. She doesn't want to be deceitful and manipulative. She doesn't want to forsake the very people she loves and cares for in order to further her career. But as that longing sweeps over her, Andy sees the truth. She sees the faces of Lilly, Emily, and Nate. She sees herself for who she truly is. And she doesn't like what she sees.

Read Ephesians 6:24. What were Paul's final words to the Ephesians in this verse?

I prayed and thought long and hard about how to end our final section together. And all I felt was a deep desire for you, the reader, and me, the writer, to love Christ with an undying love. But how do we attain such a great adoration? How do we achieve it? We know the mistakes Andy makes, the distractions she allows to slowly separate her from those she loves. We know the Ephesians' story and the demise of their affections. We know the temporality of their love, how easily they became distracted by other things. So how do we avoid their downfall?

Read Ephesians 6:21–22. In verse 22 Paul lists two reasons for why he sent Tychicus to the Ephesians. What was the final reason?

____

____

____

Several months ago I befriended a non-Christian. She's a sweet lady, and though my family and I have repeatedly shared the gospel with her and her family, she's not been open to receiving Christ. Lately, my friendship with her has been a struggle. I've always viewed encounters with her as a missionary endeavor. But recently, I've acknowledged the fact that this relationship does nothing to encourage me in my love for the Lord. If anything, it has become a hindrance.

I've had to distance myself lately in order to spend time with my friends who are in pursuit of a deeper relationship with the Lord. I've been immersing myself in their presence, allowing my passion for Christ to be strengthened through their enthusiasm. I need them, they're my Tychicus. They encourage me in my faith, and I do the same for them.

Do you have a Tychicus–someone who encourages you in your walk with the Lord? If so, who?

____

____

An undying love does not occur in isolation. It is fostered and nurtured through the encouragement of other Christians. It is a love set ablaze by Christ himself and rekindled by the spirit of God in other believers.

In Ephesians 6:23, Paul concludes his letter by bestowing a blessing. He wishes his brothers and sisters at Ephesus a fond farewell by asking that God would grant them peace and love with faith.

In addition to the encouragement of other Christians, we need something else in order to profess an undying love for the Lord. We need the Lord and all he has to offer. We need him. We need to receive his love for us. We also need to receive the faith he's given in order to maintain our relationship with him.

Our love for Christ is not one-sided. It's not mustered from some inner sense of obligation. Our relationship with Christ is in response to his initiatives. He pursues us with his love and faithfulness, and along the way he equips us with the love and faith we need to respond to his love. He is the object of our affection, but he's also the one who endows us with the love we need to truly love him in return.

So if this is the case, if Christ initiates a relationship with us and then equips us with the love and faith we need to maintain that relationship, then why do you think the Ephesians lost their first love?

____

____

____

____

____

____

Andy sits at a table in the corner of the restaurant, a view of the New York streets before her. She is disinterested in the menu. Today, the only meal she will be eating is crow. She needs to apologize to Nate. After all she's done to hurt him, at the very least, she owes him an apology.

Nate approaches the table with indifference, informing her he has little time for their meeting. Okay, she probably deserves that terse greeting. But she won't let it deter her. She needs to tell him the truth. He's right; she had forsaken him and the others she loved.

The words don't come quickly, but much to Andy's relief they come nonetheless. Nate's first response is sarcasm. But when Andy replies with an earnest apology, his features relax a little. His eyes blink and when they reopen there is kindness there. A faint smile reaches the corners of his mouth, and Andy knows there is forgiveness in his heart.

Do you know what an undying love is? In my opinion, it isn't a love that never makes mistakes or fails to fall for distractions. An undying love is a love that never gives up. A love that gets distracted, receives correction, learns from mistakes, and keeps on going.

The book of Revelation records the last known account of the Ephesians' relationship with the Lord in chapter 2. We've mentioned this account previously. But who says that's all there is to the story? Who says they never remembered and repented? Who says they never ate a little crow and gave Christ an earnest apology? Most likely, they offered a response to Christ's reprimand. Possibly, the Ephesians had some type of reaction to John's letter to the seven churches. And if they saw their name and their discretion among John's writings, surely they must have formulated a response. So how do we really know the Ephesians' relationship ended with that reprimand? Most likely, it didn't.

Write Romans 15:4 below.

____

____

____

____

The Ephesians' relationship with the Savior teaches us what to do and what not to do in our walk with the Lord. Though the Bible does not reveal the final ending to the Ephesians' love affair with Christ, there is something that it does reveal. It gives us an honest glimpse into a long-term relationship with the Lord. It allows us the opportunity to see the failure and folly of human affection and the undying love of Christ.

Christ is in this relationship for the long haul. He has no intention of failing us, no desire to dispose of us. He loves us with an everlasting love. And I'm encouraged to know that there were others in history who attempted to love him in return. They may have tried and failed and tried again, but their endurance encourages me and gives me hope.

Without God's help, we could never love Christ with an undying love. But through him and the transforming nature of his Spirit, all things are possible. So let's go ahead and trust him and take our best shot at undying love–because we know he'll help us along the way. And if we fail on occasion, we know he'll be there to remind us that we've lost our focus. Thank God for those sweet reprimands, for in the end, I believe they'll lead us to an undying love for the Savior.

Prayer–*Lord, I pray that our love for you is sincere and undying. Allow us to receive your love and faithfulness so that in return, we might love you more fully. Give us a Tychicus who encourages us in our relationship with you. And as you write our love affair upon the pages of history, may our relationship be a tale of undying love.*